INTRODUCTION TO ACCOUNTING

Economics

Editor
SIR ROY HARROD
F B A

Hon. Student of Christ Church, Oxford,
and Hon. Fellow of Nuffield College

By the same author

National Income and Social Accounting
(with Professor Alan T. Peacock and Ronald Cooper)

Business Budgets and Accounts

INTRODUCTION TO
ACCOUNTING

Harold C. Edey

Professor of Accounting at the London School
of Economics and Political Science
in the University of London

HUTCHINSON UNIVERSITY LIBRARY
LONDON

HUTCHINSON & CO (*Publishers*) LTD
178–202 Great Portland Street, London W.1

London Melbourne Sydney
Auckland Bombay Toronto
Johannesburg New York

First published 1963
Second edition 1964
Reprinted 1966, 1967 and 1969

This book has been set in Times, printed in Great Britain
on Smooth Wove paper by Anchor Press, and
bound by Wm. Brendon, both of Tiptree, Essex

09 067401 4 (cased)

09 067403 0 (paper)

CONTENTS

5

PREFACE

THIS book is based on an introductory course in accounting given at the London School of Economics and Political Science. It is designed in accordance with my view that anyone who wishes to learn something of accounting, whether he intends to go on to more advanced studies or whether he is learning the subject as a background to studies in business finance, economics, operational research, or management generally, requires an introduction that will give him a good grounding in the principles without taking him far into detailed applications. Nor does the beginner need a description of systems of original records that have now virtually disappeared in these days of accounting machines and electronic computers.

I have attempted to provide a foundation on which can be built any kind of accounting, from the traditional form typical of earlier days to the most advanced computer-operated data processing system. At the same time I have attempted to draw the student's attention to the fact that accounting data are collected only in order to be of use to management, shareholders, or others.

The main concern of this book is with the technique of handling accounting data. It is not possible, however, to write a book on accounting without mentioning valuation conventions. I have not attempted to provide a detailed criticism of existing conventions (this I hope to do in a later work), but I have drawn attention to their provisional nature and suggested that improvement may be possible. I have also inserted some examples and exercises which draw attention to the care that must be used when interpreting accounting data or employing them for the purpose of making economic decisions. I hope that this will enable students to enter into the study of more advanced problems with a healthy scepticism.

The level of approach is that appropriate to undergraduate or graduate courses in universities and colleges of technology. It represents about one term's work. Part I, covering the basic ideas of the balance sheet and profit and loss acccount, and of double entry, is complete in itself. Part II may be regarded as supplementary: it contains one chapter on the data flow system (replacing the traditional sections on books of original entry), and one on the interpretation of final accounts.

I owe a debt to Sir Roy Harrod for reading the book and offering valuable criticisms. He is of course not responsible for my errors of commission and omission.

I should also like to thank Miss Patricia Harwood who typed it.

PART I

BALANCE SHEETS, PROFIT AND LOSS ACCOUNTS AND DOUBLE ENTRY

THE BALANCE SHEET

The general nature of the balance sheet

The balance sheet is a device for describing an economic situation in a systematic standard form. By putting economic information into this form it is possible to tell a complicated story in less time and space than if the same story were written out as an extended narrative.

It is useful to distinguish between actual balance sheets and the idea of the balance sheet as a framework to help us to formulate in our minds an orderly picture of a real or assumed economic situation.

Actual balance sheets are intended to relate to real economic situations. This must not be taken to mean, however, that 'economic reality' is something we can express without reference to personal views. When human beings discuss or think about economic matters, or try to assess economic magnitudes, the expression of economic reality can only be based on assumptions and estimates made by particular persons with respect to particular economic events or situations. For this reason the balance sheet and other accounting statements can seldom be 'right' in an absolute sense: views differ. In many situations, however, there is sufficient general agreement among those interested to make it worthwhile to set down the agreed or nearly agreed facts in schematic – e.g. in balance sheet – form.

One of the main problems of the accountant is, or should be, to bring his statements into as close a relation with economic reality, in the above sense, as possible.

The balance sheet is the fundamental statement of accounting. All other accounting statements – notably the profit and loss statement – are in essence derived either from a balance sheet or from a comparison of two balance sheets at different points of time.[1]

A balance sheet is essentially an ordered statement of:

1 a set of economic resources or *assets*, each with a value set upon it; and
2 the financial claims of persons on the fund of value represented by these assets.[2]

Since all assets are, by definition, owned by someone, the total claims just exhaust the value of the assets. Another way of describing the claims is to say that they represent the way in which the holding of the assets is being *financed*.

Let us consider an individual *A*. Let us suppose that his private balance sheet at a given moment of time is as follows:

Assets

	£
House	4,000
Investments	500
Cash (money)[3]	50
	4,550

1 We must emphasize that this does not mean that all such statements are derived from conventional balance sheets of the kind prepared, for example, for submission to company shareholders. We mean that the preparation of all accounting statements implies, *inter alia*, a process of listing assets and liabilities, and setting values on these.

2 'Persons' here includes organizations.

3 Accountants usually call all money 'cash', whether in the form of coin, notes, bank balances, or cheques not yet paid into the bank. Coin and notes held for minor payments are called 'petty cash'.

Claims or finance

	£
Owing to a friend	1,500
Ownership interest (wealth)	3,050
	4,550

This balance sheet shows:

1 The assets owned by A, and the money values set on these: in total £4,550.
2 The amount owing by A to third parties: in other words the claims of third parties against A: £1,500. These are called A's *liabilities*.
3 A's residual claim on the assets, the difference between 1 and 2: £3,050. This is the net value of all A's property after what he owes to other people has been deducted. We shall call this A's *ownership interest*. Other terms that can be used are wealth, capital, ownership claim, equity.

Usually one would expect A's assets to be greater than the claims against them (apart from his own residual ownership interest). If the reverse were true, A's wealth would be negative; he would then, at the time of the balance sheet, owe more than he could pay, always assuming that the assets were shown at the value which they would fetch if they were sold. In these circumstances he would be *insolvent* and might be made bankrupt if he were suddenly called upon to pay his debts.

An important thing to notice about the balance sheet is that it always balances: that is to say, the total value of the assets is always equal to the total value of the claims or finance. This is because the ownership interest always makes up the difference between the asset values and the liabilities to outsiders. The amount of the owner's interest shown in the balance sheet depends upon the assessment made by A, or by his accountant, of the value of the assets and of the amount of the liabilities. In practice this assessment often raises problems. However, for the time being we shall avoid these in order to concentrate upon the nature of the balance sheet and of the other statements that can be derived from it. We shall assume for the time being that the assets in the balance sheet, other than cash, are taken at their saleable value, and that the liabilities are stated at the amount needed to pay them off.

Finance

The balance sheet demonstrates that for every economic resource that A possesses, someone must provide finance: in other words, the total value of the assets held by A represents the provision of finance of exactly equal amount, either by A himself, or by outsiders, or by both. A can only hold assets amounting to £4,550 if he himself, or creditors to whom he owes money, or both, are prepared to forgo spending money on other things. This apparently trivial statement is of great economic importance. It draws attention, first to the deliberate choice made by A to have the particular collection of assets shown in his balance sheet rather than to spend the money he could get by selling these on personal consumption or on a different collection of assets; and secondly to an important limiting factor in all economic affairs, namely that control of additional economic resources can only be obtained if someone is prepared (or is forced) to sacrifice for the time being the disposition of purchasing power that he could otherwise have enjoyed.

Let us now suppose that A wants to buy a cottage costing £500. His balance sheet shows that, except for the £50, he has no ready money. If he does not want to sell some of his investments, he can have the cottage only if extra finance is provided by someone else.

This can be expressed schematically by showing his balance sheet as it would appear if he bought the cottage. The cottage and the new finance are shown in italics. We have:

Assets

	£
House	4,000
Investments	500
Cash	50
Cottage	*500*
	5,050

Finance

	£
Owing to friend	1,500
Ownership interest	3,050
New finance needed	*500*
	5,050

By putting the cottage among the assets we have created a gap in the claims section of the balance sheet which must be filled by new finance. If someone gives A a present of £500, this new finance will become part of A's ownership interest: he can then finance the cottage himself. If he borrows the money, the new finance represents an additional liability of A to a building society or a bank or someone else. Whoever provides the money will have to forgo possible expenditure that he could otherwise have incurred (unless the money is borrowed, in turn, from someone else).

Transaction analysis

Let us now return to A's original balance sheet (i.e. before the cottage was bought) and examine the effect of some transactions over a period of time. Let us assume the balance sheet was drawn up on Wednesday night. On Thursday A spends £20 on food and entertainment. His cash will therefore fall by £20. He has gained no other asset.[1]

The new balance sheet, on Thursday night, will be:

Assets

	£
House	4,000
Investments	500
Cash	30
	4,530

1 In a sense, of course, A has acquired an asset, since his personal pleasure is increased; but this asset is presumably of short durability. For practical purposes it is ignored.

Finance

	£
Creditors	1,500
Ownership	3,030
	4,530

The effect of this change is to reduce the total claim by *A* himself against the assets, that is his ownership interest, by £20. This now appears as £3,030 instead of £3,050.

On Friday, let us say, *A* receives £150 in respect of his salary for the month, and he repays £100 of the £1,500 he owes to his friend. The net effect of these two transactions on his cash will be to increase it by £50. He now owes £100 less to his creditor, however. Hence his ownership interest has risen by more than the amount of the net increase in cash. It has in fact risen by £150.

On Saturday *A* spends £10 on food and entertainment and £40 on improving the house. As £40 out of the £50 spent may be assumed to increase the value of the house, *A*'s ownership interest only falls by £10, the amount spent on the benefits that are assumed to have disappeared as soon as they have been enjoyed. The net decrease in his cash it is true is £50; but the asset 'house' rises by £40; and his ownership interest falls only by the difference, £10.

His balance sheets on the four consecutive days will read as follows:

	Wed £	Thurs £	Fri £	Sat £
House	4,000	4,000	4,000	4,040
Investments	500	500	500	500
Cash	50	30	80	30
	4,550	4,530	4,580	4,570
Creditors	1,500	1,500	1,400	1,400
Ownership interest	3,050	3,030	3,180	3,170
	4,550	4,530	4,580	4,570

Here we have a set of statements summarizing what has happened to *A*'s finances during this period. These tell the tale much more quickly and concisely than is possible in words.

Flow of funds

A slightly different picture can be given if, instead of the actual balance sheets, we show the differences in each class of asset and in each source of finance, between succeeding balance sheets:

	Wed– Thurs £	Thurs– Fri £	Fri– Sat £	Wed– Sat £
House	—	—	+40	+ 40
Investments	—	—	—	—
Cash	−20	+50	−50	− 20
	−20	+50	−10	+ 20
Creditors	—	−100	—	−100
Ownership interest	−20	+150	−10	+120
	−20	+ 50	−10	+ 20

A statement of this kind, showing the period-to-period changes in assets and finance, is called a *statement of sources and uses of funds* or, more shortly, a *flow of funds statement*. It provides a summary of the way in which finance has been made available and how it has been used.

We can also derive from the figures a statement that summarizes *A*'s cash flows. This is a particularly important form of statement, because cash, the accountant's term for money, is an asset that can be used immediately for any purpose, whereas before the finance locked up in other assets can be released they must be sold or bartered. Sale or barter usually takes time; furthermore, the purchasing power realized by the sale or barter tends to be less, the shorter the time allowed for the transaction, i.e. the quicker the deal has to be put through. The statement of *A*'s cash flows can be summarized as follows:

	Wed– Thurs £	Thurs– Fri £	Fri– Sat £	Wed– Sat £
Receipts	—	150	—	150
less Payments	20	100	50	170
Change in balance[1]	− 20	+ 50	− 50	− 20

1 The balance is the amount held at a given time.

Income and expenditure

We can extract other sets of figures that are of special financial and economic significance. First of all we can note each day the net gain in resources that *A* has received as a result of his daily occupation. In our example this is given by his salary. We call this *A*'s *income*. Secondly, we can show his expenditure on *consumption*: the amount he has spent on the purchase of such things as food, clothing, entertainment. Thirdly, we can show his *saving*. This is a residue, the difference between his income and his expenditure on consumption. It represents the increase in his wealth or ownership interest. On days when the expenditure exceeds income this will be negative, as shown in the following table. On the first line is the income, on the second the expenditure on consumption, and on the third the saving or dissaving for the period – the change in wealth:

	Wed–Thurs £	Thurs–Fri £	Fri–Sat £	Wed–Sat £
Income	—	150	—	150
less Expenditure on consumption	20	—	10	30
Saving = change in ownership interest or wealth	−20	+150	−10	+120

The figures in the final line of this table are the same as those in the 'ownership interest' line of the flow of funds statement. The former can, therefore, be regarded as explaining certain balance sheet changes. The figures we are using at present are so simple that this analysis may seem of relatively little importance, since anyone could pick out these points without using special tables. This is far from being the case, however, in a large organization; and even in relatively uncomplicated personal circumstances it is often both revealing and helpful to summarize significant figures in a systematic way as we have done here. The table showing income, expenditure on consumption, and saving, focuses attention on three important economic aspects of *A*'s behaviour. All three figures are obviously of relevance to him. To students of economics who wish to study the aggregate effect of the transactions of all the A's in the country they are of great importance.[1]

The financial statements we have discussed in this chapter are typical of the statements that, in one form or another, are used throughout business and in public departments and organizations. When we study business statements we shall find that some of the classifications differ a little from those in this chapter; but there will be no great difference in essentials. In the next chapter we shall examine the kind of statements that are used in the analysis of simple business transactions.

[1] The example in this chapter has been devised to make A's expenditure on consumption and saving tally with the definitions used in national statistics.

THE BUSINESS BALANCE SHEET.
DOUBLE ENTRY BOOK-KEEPING

Business transactions

We shall now apply the type of analysis used in Chapter 1 to business transactions.

Our first example will be a small retail business. We shall assume it is managed by the owner, who rents the shop and employs one assistant. Our aim will be to summarize the economic position of the business at various times, and to analyse the transactions leading to changes in this position. The accounting statements will relate to the business only: they will exclude the owner's private affairs, and any other business activities that he carries on. This is an important point: the set of activities covered by accounting records and reports must always be clearly defined.

We shall record one week's transactions, from one Saturday night to the following Saturday night.[1] The opening figures, which show the business's economic position at the beginning of the period, and the transactions during the period, are as follows:

Opening figures, showing position on the first Saturday night:

	£
Stock of goods for sale ('stock' or 'stock in trade'), valued at the prices at which the goods were originally bought	100
Owing by customers ('trade debtors') to whom goods have been sold	20
Money in the bank ('cash at bank')	140
Owing to suppliers ('trade creditors') from whom goods have been bought	150
Ownership interest	110

1 Balance sheets are not usually made up every day – except perhaps, in an approximate way, by banks and similar organizations. But a daily analysis is better for illustration.

Transactions:

Monday	a	Sold for £25, paid at once, a quantity of stock that originally cost £20; paid the £25 into the bank.
	b	Owner withdrew £10 from the bank for personal use. (Such withdrawals from the business by the owner are called *drawings*, unless it is a limited company; then they are called *dividends*.)
Tuesday	c	As for *a*.
	d	Paid creditors £150 by sending them cheques drawn on the business bank account.
Wednesday	e	As for *a*.
	f	Bought stock costing £160, on one week's credit (i.e. payment is not due to the suppliers until next Tuesday).
	g	Bought stock costing £40 for cash (i.e. payment is due at once), payment being by cheque.
Thursday	h	As for *a*.
Friday	i	Sold stock that originally cost £40 for £50 in cash, and paid this into the bank.
	i	Received the amount owing from the trade debtors, £20, and paid this into the bank.
Saturday	k	Sold stock that originally cost £36 for £45 in cash and paid this into the bank.
		Sold stock that originally cost £24 for £30, on one week's credit.
	m	Paid one week's rent of the shop, £10, by cheque.
	n	Paid the assistant's weekly wages, £12, by cheque.

The first step in the analysis is to put the opening figures into balance sheet form. We have, first, three classes of assets:

	£
Stock	100
Trade debtors	20
Cash at bank	140
	260

We have one class of non-ownership claims or liabilities:

Trade creditors   £150

It follows that the trader's ownership interest is the difference, £110. We shall not use the term 'wealth' as an alternative to ownership interest, for we are now only concerned with that part of the owner's wealth that relates to this business; his private wealth, and any interests in other businesses, are excluded. The term 'ownership interest' can now be interpreted as the claim the owner – now distinct from the business organization – has on the business. This is sometimes called the 'capital' of the business. When the business is under the control of a manager who runs it on behalf of the owner, the ownership interest can also be regarded as the value of the economic resources entrusted to the manager by the owner at the date of the balance sheet.

The position at the close of business on the first Saturday night is summarized in balance sheet form in the first column of Table 2.1.

TABLE 2.1

BALANCE SHEETS

£

	Sat	Mon	Tues	Wed	Thurs	Fri	Sat
Assets							
Stock	100	80	60	240	220	180	120
Trade debtors	20	20	20	20	20	—	30
Cash at bank	140	155	30	15	40	110	133
Total assets	260	255	110	275	280	290	283
Finance							
Trade creditors	150	150	—	160	160	160	160
Ownership interest:							
At beginning of week	110	100	100	100	100	100	100
Profit during week	—	5	10	15	20	30	23
Total ownership interest	110	105	110	115	120	130	123
Total finance	260	255	110	275	280	290	283

The net changes from day to day, and for the whole week, can be summarized conveniently in a flow of funds statement. This is shown in Table 2.2. This gives us a clear and systematic picture of the changes in the structure of assets and finance during the week.

It will be instructive to work through the transactions, noting how the changes in the balance sheet arise.

TABLE 2.2

FLOW OF FUNDS

£

	Sat–Mon	Mon–Tues	Tues–Wed	Wed–Thurs	Thurs–Fri	Fri–Sat	Week
Stock	− 20	− 20	+180	− 20	− 40	− 60	+ 20
Trade debtors	—	—	—	—	− 20	+ 30	+ 10
Cash at bank	+ 15	−125	− 15	+ 25	+ 70	+ 23	− 7
	− 5	− 145	+165	+ 5	+ 10	− 7	+ 23
Trade creditors	—	−150	+160	—	—	—	+ 10
Ownership interest							
At beginning of week	− 10	—	—	—	—	—	− 10
Profit during week	+ 5	+ 5	+ 5	+ 5	+ 10	− 7	+ 23
	− 5	−145	+165	+ 5	+ 10	− 7	+ 23

We start with transaction *a*, on Monday. This causes an asset, stock, to be reduced by £20. At the same time another asset, cash at bank, rises by £25. The difference is profit: we have sold something valued at £20 for £25. There is thus a net rise in assets of £5: the ownership interest must rise by the same amount; the business has more value and, as if it were, owes the owner £5 more. This is recorded in a separate line in the table in order to draw attention, in terms of profit or loss, to the result of the business transactions for the week.

The reader should notice that the amount of profit recorded depends upon (1) the amount received (or receivable) for the goods sold, and (2) the balance sheet value set upon the stock just before it is sold. As the stock originally cost £20 and was sold for £25 it can be assumed that the business operations have raised its value by the difference. It would not have been unreasonable, if the sale was confidently expected, to increase the value of the stock, and record the corresponding increase in ownership interest – the profit – *before* it was sold. The normal accounting convention, however, is to follow the procedure shown in the table: profit is not acknowledged in the balance sheet until an actual sale provides external evidence of the increased value of the stock.

This illustrates a point made earlier: that actual balance sheets do not necessarily correspond with economic reality. Two points may be made in justification of the convention. First, personal opinions normally play an important part in valuations: it must not be assumed that there is always a unique valuation figure. Secondly, the everyday routine of accounting calls for clearly defined rules of valuation which will convey a reasonable amount of information and can be applied without undue uncertainty. It must be admitted, however, that accounting procedures sometimes depart much further from *any* reasonable estimate of economic reality than is desirable. We shall return to this question later, noting here the practical conclusion that for some purposes the figures in accounts must be regarded only as a kind of rough memorandum of value or value changes, and must be examined, and if necessary adjusted, before they are used for business calculations.

We now return to our analysis. The second transaction on Monday, *b*, represents a fall in an asset, cash, and an equivalent fall in the ownership interest: the business has, as it were, satisfied part of this claim by sacrificing cash to the owner. Here the ownership claim changes, but this is *not* due to profit or loss.

The net effect of the two transactions on Monday appears in the first column of Table 2.2. When the figures in this column are applied to the appropriate figures in the first column of Table 2.1 we obtain the second column of Table 2.1. Readers should check that this is true.

The first transaction on Tuesday, *c*, is a repetition of *a*. Transaction *d*, however, is of a new type. It represents a change in balance sheet structure, but does not affect the ownership claim. Creditors have been paid and cash sacrificed in the process: we have a fall in outside claims against the business and a fall in assets. In transaction *a*, on the other hand, there was both a change in asset structure – stock into cash – *and* a net increase in the ownership claim.

The net effect of Tuesday's transactions is a fall in assets of

£145, a fall in outside claims of £150, and an increase in the ownership claim by £5, as Table 2.2 shows.

On Wednesday we have first a repetition, in *e*, of Monday's transaction *a*. Then *f*, an additional asset, stock, is acquired in exchange for acceptance of a liability – that is, of an outside claim against the business – of £160. We value the stock at the same figure, so that assets and outside claims both rise by £160. A further addition to stock is made, *g*, the consideration being an immediate cash payment of £40. Thus in one case additional assets are acquired by accepting additional claims against the business: that is, the immediate finance is provided from outside the business; in the other case the business itself, by sacrificing cash, provides the finance internally. The flow of funds statement in Table 2.2 brings out the net effect of the three transactions: the information that has required a paragraph of writing appears in the table in a form that can be understood and absorbed at a single glance.

Thursday's transaction, *h*, is again a repetition of *a*. It appears in the fourth column of Table 2.2.

On Friday there is a transaction, *i*, similar to *a*, but involving a larger sum: the end of the week is bringing increasing activity. On the same day, trade debtors amounting to £20 are replaced by cash: this is another balance sheet structure change that does not affect profit. Its effect is, however, to make the business more liquid, as it is said: cash can be spent at once; the amount owing in the form of trade debts cannot be spent until it is collected.[1]

Any change in the structure of assets and liabilities of a business, whether or not there is also a change in the ownership interest, may alter the liquidity of the business, that is, may affect the cash it holds or its ability to obtain cash in the sense that it may change (1) the speed with which it can obtain a given cash sum, and (2) the amount of asset value it must sacrifice, if any, in order to obtain the cash sooner rather than later. Thus, transaction *i*, in which stock was sold for cash, represented *both*

---

1 It is sometimes possible to sell debts to a third party, or borrow on the security of debts, before they are due, but in such cases a sacrifice of part of the value of the debt has to be made – i.e. as 'discount' or 'interest' – as the price of this.

a profitable transaction *and* a movement towards increased liquidity.[1]

The net effect of Friday's transactions appears in the fifth column of Table 2.2.

On Saturday we have, first, a sales transaction, k, like a. Next there is another sales transaction, l, in which a debt is accepted instead of cash in exchange for the stock. In business language k is called a *cash sale*, l a *credit sale*; in both cases there is a fall in an asset (stock), a rise in another asset (in one case cash, in the other trade debtors), and a rise in the ownership interest (profit). Next we have two transactions, m and n, in each of which there is a fall in an asset (cash) but no corresponding increase in another asset and no fall in a liability. Instead there is, in both cases, a fall in the ownership interest. These falls are not due to withdrawal of money value from the business by the owner, as in b: they are incurred as part of the process of running the business. They are an offset against the profit and are called *expenses*. Thus, unlike drawings, which transfer value to the owner, expenses reduce the profit: the amounts in question have been spent in the course of the business activity. The ownership interest is thereby reduced, though no doubt in the hope that the sum of such sacrifices in any period will be more than offset by the profit margin earned by the sales.[2]

Saturday's transactions are summarized in the sixth column of Table 2.2.

Double entry book-keeping

As we found before, our verbal description has been lengthy

1 If the stock had been sold quickly in order to obtain increased liquidity, it might have been necessary to accept a lower price (and therefore lower profit) than if it was sold more slowly.

2 As we shall see later, however, some outlays of this kind are assumed to create an asset of equivalent value. It is to some extent a matter of convention, merely affecting the time when profits and losses are recorded, what payments are assumed to give rise to immediate profit reductions (expenses) and what are considered to create equivalent assets as when stock is bought. If payments like wages are treated as if they raised the value of stock by an equivalent amount, the profit is not reduced at the moment of the outlay; the profit shown at the moment when the stock is sold is then correspondingly smaller, as the recorded value of the stock is then higher.

and troublesome to follow; yet we are dealing here with only a few transactions of the simplest kind: in business, and in public affairs, the complications can be very great. We have seen how accounting statements – the balance sheets and the flow of funds statements – summarize the data in a convenient form. A systematic way of collecting and classifying the extensive original data which are to be summarized and presented in these statements is also required. This is provided by the double entry system of book-keeping.[1] In its essentials the system consists of a set of statistical tables or *ledger accounts*,[2] one for each class of asset or claim. The figures in each such table are so arranged as to form a continuous record of the value initially recorded and the subsequent changes in value. Furthermore, in order to facilitate arithmetical control, a system of recording is used which in essence amounts to treating assets and claims as of opposite algebraic sign.

The fundamental ideas of the system are illustrated in Table 2.3. In this table the original numerical information from the example at the beginning of this chapter is analysed into the appropriate balance sheet classifications. There is a column for each type of asset and for each type of claim: these columns are the ledger accounts; they are numbered from (1) to (6). Each ledger account has a left-hand side (which we may call the + side) and a right-hand side (which we may call the – side). These are also called, respectively, the *debit* and the *credit* sides, and we shall henceforth use these traditional terms. It is important to realize that the terms 'debit' and 'credit' as they are used in accounting have a purely technical meaning. The reader should put out of his mind firmly any previous conception that debit necessarily implies loss and that credit necessarily implies gain. The accounting meaning of these terms is given in the

1 The traditional word 'book-keeping' now includes mechanical and electronic systems of records. The term *data processing* is tending, in consequence, to replace it.

2 The term 'ledger account' is derived from the traditional ledger or book in which double entry accounts were kept. The name no longer implies the existence of a book, only of a systematic collection of numerical records. For reading on the historical origins of the ledger, see Littleton and Yamey (editors), *Studies in the History of Accounting* (London, 1956).

statement of the rules of the double entry system in the next paragraph. This statement is a *definition* of debit and credit: it is from the statement that the terms derive their meaning in this book.[1]

The fundamental rules of the double entry system are as follows:

> *Assets* and *increases in assets* are entered as *positive* (+) items and are called *debits*.
>
> *Claims* and *increases in claims* are entered as *negative* (−) items and are called *credits*.
>
> *Decreases in assets* are entered as *negative* (−) items and are called *credits*.
>
> *Decreases in claims* are entered as *positive* (+) items and are called *debits*.

It follows from the definition of assets and claims that any change in one account must always be accompanied by a change of opposite sign in another account or, to use the traditional language, *every debit has its credit*.[2]

Thus we may have:

An increase in an asset (debit) accompanied by:

> (*a*) an equal increase in a claim (credit), *or*
> (*b*) an equal decrease in another asset (credit).

An increase in a claim (credit) accompanied by:

> (*a*) an equal increase in an asset (debit), *or*
> (*b*) an equal decrease in another claim (debit).

A decrease in an asset (credit) accompanied by:

> (*a*) an equal decrease in a claim (debit), *or*
> (*b*) an equal increase in another asset (debit).

A decrease in a claim (debit) accompanied by:

> (*a*) an equal decrease in an asset (credit), *or*
> (*b*) an equal increase in another claim (credit).

These rules are invariable. It should be noted, however, that in practice it is often convenient, when recording items, to merge

1 The appendix to this chapter contains a further discussion of the significance of the two terms.

2 The opposite side of a given entry – the debit corresponding to a given credit or *vice versa* – is sometimes called the *contra* entry or simply 'the contra'.

more than one entry together, so that, for example, one debit entry may be matched by several credit entries which sum to the same amount; and so on.

Let us apply these rules in Table 2.3. In Column (1) we have, on

TABLE 2.3

DOUBLE ENTRY ANALYSIS

Asset increases and claim decreases (debits) appear on left-hand side of accounts. Claim increases and asset decreases (credits) appear on right-hand side of accounts.

	(1) Stock Dr +£	Cr −£	(2) Trade debtors Dr +£	Cr −£	(3) Cash at bank Dr +£	Cr −£	(4) Trade creditors Dr +£	Cr −£	(5) Capital Dr +£	Cr −£	(6) Profit and loss Dr +£	Cr −£
Opening balances	100		20		140			150		110		
Monday												
a		20			25							5
b						10			10			
Tuesday												
c		20			25							5
d						150	150					
Wednesday												
e		20			25							5
f	160							160				
g	40					40						
Thursday												
h		20			25							5
Friday												
i		40			50							10
j				20	20							
Saturday												
k		36			45							9
l		24	30									6
m							10			10		
n							12			12		
	300	180	50	20	355	222	150	310	10	110	22	45
Closing balances[1]	120		30		133			160		100		23

1 Net differences between debit and credit items. If the debit total is greater than the credit total in any column, the balance must appear on the debit side; and contrariwise, if the credit total is the greater. The closing balances of one period are the opening balances of the next.

the first line, the stock at the beginning of the period, the *opening balance*. This is £100, the balance sheet value at that time. The first transaction, *a*, is the sale of stock, valued at £20, for £25. This can be regarded, for balance sheet analysis, as a combination of two transactions. The first is the conversion of £20 of asset value in stock into another asset, cash. The second is an addition of £5 to asset value (cash) with an equal increase in the ownership interest (profit). The reduction of £20 in stock is entered on the credit side of the stock account. The second part of the double entry is a corresponding debit of £20 in the cash account in Column (3), for the increase in cash; this is not shown separately, but appears as part of a cash receipt of £25; the remaining £5 of the latter is the debit corresponding to a £5 credit in the profit and loss account (Column (6)): this is the profit margin and represents an increase in the ownership claim. This is an example of the amalgamation of two pairs of debits and credits: the two debits, both to the cash account, sum to £25 and are shown as one item; the two credits, one to stock account and one to the profit and loss account, similarly sum to £25.

At the close of business on Monday the sums of the items on the two sides of the stock account are £100 and £20, the debit side being greater than the credit side. The arithmetical difference is £80. This difference is called a *debit balance* of £80. A balance must always be given a sign: that is, it must be described as debit or credit. If we wished, we could draw a line across the account at this point (as at the bottom of the table) and start again with a fresh opening balance of £80 on the debit side and nothing on the credit side.

The significance of the remaining items in the stock account can be analysed in the same way. The final line of this account shows £120 as the debit balance at the end of the period: this closing balance is the balance sheet value of stock at that date, and is the opening balance of the next period.

The next column, (2), is the trade debtors account.[1] We start with the balance sheet value at the beginning of the period: this is the opening debit balance, £20. This remains unchanged until Friday, when the debts are paid (*j*). The asset then falls by £20: in other words there is a credit entry of £20, reducing the balance

1 'Trade debtors' is here used as an adjective qualifying 'account': hence we do not use an apostrophe after the final *s* of debtors.

of the account to zero. The corresponding debit is found in the cash account in Column (3): the decrease in the asset debtors (a credit) has been offset by an increase in the asset cash (a debit).

On Saturday more debts are acquired, amounting to £30, and there is a debit entry of this amount. This is the sum of two items, £24 (the other side of the transaction being the fall in stock in Column (1)) and £6 (the other side being a rise in profit in Column (6)).

There are no more items in this account; the closing balance of the trade debtors account is therefore £30 debit.

The changes in the cash account can be similarly analysed.

Ledger account (4) is concerned not with an asset or class of assets but with trade creditors, a class of claims. The opening balance is £150, and being a claim on the business this is a credit, or negative, balance. This is unchanged until Tuesday. On that day the creditors are paid (d). The creditors balance is then reduced by £150 and the cash balance falls by the same amount: reduction in a claim is accompanied by reduction in an asset. The balance of trade creditors is now zero. On Wednesday fresh claims are incurred, of £160 (f). This requires a credit entry, and there is a corresponding debit entry in the stock account, recording the increase in stock.

There are no more changes in the trade creditors account, the final balance of which is therefore £160 credit.

We now come to ledger accounts (5) and (6). These too are concerned with a claim. This claim, however, is not in respect of a liability, as was the claim of Column (4); we are now concerned with the ownership interest. It is important to maintain this distinction, for although the double entry rules for both types of claim are the same, the economic significance is different.[1] The ownership claim is here divided for convenience into two accounts, one containing the ownership interest at the beginning of the week and the ownership drawings during the week, and the other containing the profit analysis. This division corresponds to the division in the balance sheets in Table 2.1. The first account we call the *capital account* (Column 5) and the second *the profit and loss account* (Column 6).

[1] Ledger accounts concerned with the ownership claim are sometimes called *nominal accounts*.

The opening balance of the capital account shows the owner-ship claim at the beginning of the week, £110. This is a credit. On Monday this claim is reduced by £10 when the owner with-draws cash (*b*). This requires a debit entry, reducing the balance to £100. The contra entry is the credit of £10 in the cash account. No other transactions between owner and business occur during the week, and we end with a credit balance of £100. (The next step might be to re-classify as capital the profit of £23 for the week in Column (6) before starting the next week, in order to show the total ownership interest at the beginning of that week. This step is not shown here; it will be introduced in later examples.)

Finally we have the profit and loss account in Column (6). This account has no opening balance, as the whole ownership interest at the beginning of the week was, in this particular example, classified as capital. On Monday there is a profit of £5, corresponding, as we have already seen, to £5 out of the increase of £25 in cash which occurs that day (*a*). The profit of £5 is therefore recorded as a credit entry in the profit and loss account. This entry is followed by a series of similar ones.

On Saturday two reductions in profit are recorded in the account as debits. These are expenses, the contra items to the cash payments for rent and wages. We thus have two debits for £10 and £12 respectively.

The credit side of the profit and loss account totals £45. The debit side totals £22. The balance at the end of the period is therefore £23 credit. As there was no opening balance this is a measure of the net profit made by the business during the week: the owner's claim on the business has risen by £23 as a result – the business 'owes' him £23 more, as it were.

Let us recapitulate. The balance sheet, and the detailed double entry records from which it is in practice extracted, can be regarded as a statement of:

(1) the resources that have been put into the hands of the top management of the business, the assets; and

(2) the claims of the various people or organizations to whom the top management is responsible for these assets, of which the claim of the owner or owners has a special significance.

The claims always equal the assets because what would other-

wise be an excess of assets over liabilities is always balanced
exactly by the ownership claim for the residue. It is one of the
jobs of the management to produce profit; but as soon as it has
been produced there is an increase in the management responsibility because of the additional net resources now in its hands.[1]

The numerical sum of the debits in a double entry system must
always equal the numerical sum of the credits: this follows from
our definitions and is an expression of the fact that the respective
totals of asset values and claims are always equal. A balance
sheet can always be extracted from the double entry records by
listing all the balances, debit and credit, as they are at a given
moment of time.[2] If we think in terms of algebraic sign, we can
say that the algebraic sum of the asset values and the claims must
always be zero. If this is found in practice not to be so, we know
there is an error in the records.

It has been traditional in book-keeping to use the left-hand
and right-hand side convention that is illustrated in Table 2.3.
This convention remains a valuable practical method of classification, and is one that all accountants use as a matter of course
when they think and write. However, it is often more convenient, in the practical work of collecting and classifying data,
to work in terms of plus and minus, particularly where mechanical or electronic devices are in use. The terms debit and credit
are always retained as well, however.[3]

It is important to note, in order to avoid possible confusion,
that the left-hand and right-hand side convention for indicating

1 When we look at the system in this way in relation to a business
which is managed by its owner, we have to distinguish the latter's
economic function as manager of the business from his function as
owner: he is, so to speak, responsible to himself in another function.
Owner-managers are not, however, typical of modern industrial
economies.

2 Entries in the double entry records must therefore always be
dated, directly or by some system of coding.

3 The algebraic signs may be reversed, + being used for credits
and − for debits. The essential point to remember is that debits and
credits have opposite algebraic signs. Debit and credit are written for
short *dr* and *cr*, as already indicated. A useful way of remembering
which side is debit and which credit is to note that 'credit' contains
the letter *r* (for *right*-hand side).

debits and credits, and the plus and minus interpretation that
we have given here are not, in general, adhered to in the
presentation to shareholders, managers, and others, of information based on the system. Thus balance sheets do not necessarily
follow the 'left-hand for debits' and 'right-hand for credits' rule.
The profit and loss report to shareholders is sometimes in a more
or less conventional double entry form; but it is just as likely to
be in some other form. Plus and minus are not commonly used
in accounting reports to identify debits and credits. In short it is
essential to distinguish between the techniques used in collecting
and classifying the data and those used in preparing reports,
based on the same data, that will convey significant economic
information.

The full description of any given ledger account includes the
word 'account': thus we have cash account, capital account,
stock account, and so on. However, it is often convenient to drop
the second word and speak simply of cash, capital, stock, etc.,
when it is clear that we are referring to the ledger accounts.

If he has not already done so, the reader is advised at this
stage to work carefully through the figures we have been dis-
cussing. He should start with the data given at the beginning of
the chapter and check each opening balance and each transaction
against the figures in Table 2.3, noting as he does this the
relationship between the classified analysis for each day in Table
2.3 and the flow of funds for each day in Table 2.2. Finally he
should check the last row of Table 2.3 with the final column of
Table 2.1 Once these relationships have been grasped the transi-
tion to more complicated problems of double entry book-keeping
should not cause much difficulty. A modern accounting system
is essentially a routine for collecting a very large number of bits
of original information, sorting these out, classifying them, and
then recording them in a set of ledger accounts that in essence,
though not in detail, are like those in Table 2.3. From these can
be prepared statements, among others, of the same type as those
in Tables 2.1 and 2.2.

APPENDIX TO CHAPTER 2

THE MEANING OF DEBIT AND CREDIT

In accounting the terms 'debit' and 'credit' have a specific, technical meaning. Unfortunately these terms are also used in everyday speech in a looser and more general way. In consequence it is not always easy, in the early stages of the study of accounting, to avoid some confusion of thought. For example, it may not be easy for a reader to appreciate why he should, when he receives a prize of £25 on his premium bonds, be expected to *debit* his cash account. He feels that a credit would be more appropriate, since he associates the word credit with gain, and debit with loss.

In fact, the popular use of the word credit in this context contains, from an accountant's viewpoint, only half the truth. In order to understand the accounting one must analyse the economic significance of the cash receipt in balance sheet terms. The recipient of the prize has experienced an increase in a certain class of asset, cash. His personal balance sheet therefore shows an increase of £25 in his assets. If there is no other change in his balance sheet, it will no longer balance, however: assets will exceed claims. This is impossible; in fact, we may say that the increase in his assets has resulted in an equal increase in his claims on assets – an increase in his capital. When this is recorded the balance sheet is once more in balance.

Thus, the recipient, if he keeps his accounts by double entry, *credits* his capital account, as a record of the increase in his total wealth (which may be regarded as an increase in the money value of the total claim on resources capable of being satisfied out of the assets he holds). He also records the increase in the asset cash, and this requires a *debit* in his cash account. The transaction requires both a credit *and* a debit, for both parts of his balance sheet are affected, assets as well as claims.

35

For those who find it easier to visualize matters of this kind in personal terms, we can illustrate debit and credit in another and older way. To do this we go back to a method used in book-keeping treatises of the sixteenth century that, nevertheless, still has significance in relation to the control of assets in modern accounting systems. It will be convenient to consider the case of a business. Let us suppose that the name of each ledger account stands for a person, who at any given moment of time either *owes* money (or something of value in terms of money) to the business whose accounts we are handling, or is *owed* money or money value by it. Thus, when we think of the cash account, we think of it as a person who receives cash from the business, looks after it, makes payments on its behalf, and is responsible to it for the balance. (Where the cash is in fact looked after by a person appointed for that purpose – the cashier – as in most businesses, the cash account does indeed reflect the money entrusted to him and can be regarded as a kind of debtors account.) If we think in this way it seems quite sensible to *debit* cash account when the business receives cash: the cash account (or the cashier, for whom it stands) *owes* this money to the business; indeed, we sometimes talk of a 'charge' to an account instead of a 'debit'. When the cashier pays money out, the account is credited, for he has now discharged his responsibility: a cash payment is therefore a *credit* to the cash account. The debit balance on the cash account shows the amount the cashier has received and has not yet spent: it is what he should have in the cash box – and this can be checked by counting. The fact that in some circumstances the cashier is also the owner of the business, or has some other function, need not affect our reasoning: the cash account is concerned with the *function* of holding money.[1] If the money is paid into the bank, we *debit* the bank, which now owes the money (we may call the account 'cash at bank'); and we credit the bank when it pays out money for the business.

1 Unfortunately this term 'cash' is now often used when it would be more appropriate to speak of 'bank'; in the text we have used 'cash at bank' where it has seemed necessary to avoid ambiguity. Coin and notes actually held by the cashier for small payments are now called 'petty cash'. Money in his hands awaiting payment into the bank is recorded as if already paid in, i.e. as a debit to the bank.

We can look on other asset accounts in a similar way. Thus a debit of £1,000 to the account for motor vehicles can be regarded as recording the receipt of £1,000 of value, in the form of the vehicles, by the person responsible for these; and if we reduce the recorded value of these, e.g. because they are partly worn out, we credit the account because value has been given up: the responsibility has been reduced.

It is easy to see that creditors' accounts can be looked at in the same way. When someone lends us money we *credit* him because he has given up value to us (cash or bank being debited); and when we repay him we *debit* him because he has received value from us (cash or bank being credited).

Finally, we can look on the accounts for the owner or owners as recording the amount owed to the owner by the business. These accounts comprise the capital account, the profit and loss account, and the sub-divisions of the latter which we shall discuss later under the names of revenue and expense accounts; these accounts taken together show the ownership interest (or claim) and changes in this. When there is a net rise in this (e.g. as the result of a sale of an asset at a profit) we can say the owner is immediately owed more by the business: he can therefore be said to give value to the business, and he must be credited. Similarly if the owner pays in money, we debit cash (the cashier or the bank has received it) and we credit the owner. If the owner withdraws cash, we debit him for now he is owed less: he has received value. If a loss is made (e.g. a cash payment is made for which no value is received), the owner is immediately owed less by the business, and we *debit* him – usually in the first instance in the profit and loss account or in one of the sections of this which we call expense accounts.

Thus we can derive the following alternative formulation of our general rule for the use of debit and credit:

Debit the account that represents the recipient of value.
Credit the account that represents the giver of value.

In interpreting this rule we must remember, however, that the owner has usually a number of accounts, the balances on which together make up the total of his interest; that a fall in total ownership value (which may be a loss) is interpreted as a receipt of value by the owner in the sense that the business thereby owes him less; and that a rise in ownership value (which may be a profit) is interpreted as a giving of value by the owner, the business thenceforth owing him more.

If value is received by one person, it must be given by another. Hence every transaction must have both a debit and a credit aspect.

This formulation can be illustrated by applying it to the first four transactions in the example on page 21.

Transaction	Debit, for value received	£	Credit, for value given	£
a	Bank	25	Stock	20
			Owner (profit and loss account)	5
b	Owner (capital account)	10	Bank	10
c	Bank	25	Stock	20
			Owner (profit and loss account)	5
d	Creditors	150	Bank	150

If the results of a transaction are regarded in this light, it becomes natural to write, for example, as a summary of transaction *a* above, 'Bank is debtor to stock and profit, £25'. This type of statement is typical of early book-keeping, and still survives, e.g. in such documents as bills rendered for goods and services, which often read: '*A* debtor to *B*, for goods supplied, £25', and so on. (This explains the contraction *dr*.)

Any reader who would like to know more about the early history of book-keeping will find much to interest him in the collection of essays by Littleton and Yamey (mentioned on p. 27). The study of some of these essays can be an active help in learning the rules of double entry, in that they show how the present-day conventions arose: knowledge of the origin of things is seldom wasted.

REPORTING TO OWNERS.
PROFIT AND LOSS AND
APPROPRIATION ACCOUNTS

Reporting to owners

We have seen how a causal analysis of the profit for a given period is built up in the double entry profit and loss account (Table 2.3, Column (6)). This analysis is the basis of the profit and loss reports such as are made to management, shareholders, tax authorities. The detailed information provided by the double entry record must usually be summarized and condensed, however, before it is ready for presentation in report form. The profit and loss account in Table 2.3, for example, can be turned into a profit and loss report by summarizing the figures for each

TABLE 3.1

PROFIT AND LOSS REPORT

£

	Sat– Mon	Mon– Tues	Tues– Wed	Wed– Thurs	Thurs– Fri	Fri– Sat	Week
Revenue							
Gross profit	5	5	5	5	10	15	45
	—	—	—	—	—	—	—
Expenditure							
Rent	—	—	—	—	—	10	10
Wages	—	—	—	—	—	12	12
	—	—	—	—	—	22	22
Profit or loss	5	5	5	5	10	—7	23

significant class of revenue and expense as in Table 3.1. Here we have the daily totals for each class of revenue and expenditure, and a summary for the whole week.[1] As noted earlier, reports of this kind need not follow the form of the conventional double entry ledger account with left-hand and right-hand entries corresponding to debit and credit items.

In ordinary language, Table 3.1 tells us that sales revenue *less* the cost of the goods sold (the difference being the *gross profit* or *gross margin*) is, for the week, £45[2]; that £10 was spent on rent and £12 on wages, so that the expenses of the business for the week amounted to £22; and that the net profit, or gain in value of the ownership claim, *so far as this was due to business transactions*, was therefore £23. The qualification is necessary, as there was a fall of £10 in the ownership interest between Saturday and Monday when the owner drew £10 from the business: *such transactions are not relevant for the profit and loss analysis.* The withdrawal of money, or the payment of money into the business by the owner, belong to a class of transactions with a different economic significance. This is so whether the withdrawal is regarded as a withdrawal of value the owner has previously paid into the business (that is, of 'capital'), or of profit subsequently earned. This distinction between the

1 Daily reports are not normal in practice; it is convenient to use them here, however, in order to illustrate principles. Where we here have daily figures, reports in practice might show monthly data.

2 The words 'cost of the goods sold' as they are used here have a technical meaning: the figure to which they refer is the cost of buying the goods that have been sold and, in relation to any particular lot of goods, measures the value at which they are entered in the balance sheet before they are sold. The total cost of goods sold is not the whole cost incurred by the business during the period. It excludes such expenses as the rent and wages in this example, which, nevertheless, the business must incur in order to be able to buy and sell goods. It is usually convenient to classify this 'cost of goods sold' or 'cost of sales' separately, because of its special significance as an expense the level of which tends to vary in direct proportion to the value of the goods sold; this is less likely to be true of other expenses. Later we shall see that the term is also used in manufacturing businesses, though with a somewhat different significance.

earning of profit and the use that is made of that profit is important.[1]

A comparison of Tables 2.3 and 3.1 will bring out the distinction between the double entry profit and loss account as part of the technical accounting system of data collection and classification, and the profit and loss statement prepared as a report to shareholders or others from the information provided by the formal data collection system. Both, however, may be called *accounts*, though the words *report* and *statement* are also used for the latter.

The form of an accounting report depends on the particular legal and economic circumstances of the organization to which it refers. Thus, balance sheets and profit statements prepared for businesses owned by single individuals (known as *sole traders*) differ in certain respects from those prepared for partnerships where a number of individuals carry on a business in common. Both differ from the accounting reports drawn up for the shareholders of limited companies. The accounting reports of nationalized industries, charitable foundations, churches, all have their special features. Apart from differences in form corresponding to differences in the legal and economic character of organizations, accounting reports also vary in form and detail according to their function. The balance sheet and profit and loss account presented annually to the shareholders of a limited company will, for example, usually contain much less detailed analysis than the reports covering the same activities presented to the top management of the company.

We shall now consider the forms usually taken by balance sheets and profit and loss statements presented to the owners of sole traders' businesses, partnership businesses, and limited companies.

Capital and profit: sole traders and partnerships

The ownership interest shown in the balance sheet in Table 2.1 was divided into two parts, giving respectively the amount of the interest at the beginning of the week, *less* the subsequent

1 This distinction is sometimes indicated by describing the use made of profit as an 'appropriation of profit', and the accounting statement recording this use as an 'appropriation account'.

drawings, and the profit. This division was maintained in the flow of funds statement in Table 2.2. Thus the reader of the balance sheet was able to distinguish between the ownership interest at the beginning of the period, less the amount withdrawn by the owner during the week, and the net profit earned by the business activities. The ownership interest at the beginning of the week might have been called the *capital* of the business.[1] In one sense of the word, the capital of a business is the whole ownership interest at the beginning of the period, *plus* any profit earned *less* any withdrawals made by the owner *plus* any payments the owner has made into the business, during the period. In this sense the capital shown in Table 2.1 on, say, Wednesday night was £115: the original capital on the first Saturday night, £110, *plus* three days' profit, £15, *less* drawings on Monday, £10. In businesses run by a sole trader the distinction between capital and profit is normally only made for the purposes of each distinct accounting year: the capital at the beginning of each accounting year is distinguished in the balance sheet from the profit of that year, but the two figures (*less* any drawings and *plus* any more capital paid in) are merged at the end of the year. Hence the capital of a sole trader at the beginning of each year is said to be the whole ownership interest at that time.

The same method of presentation may be used in partnerships. More often, perhaps, a distinction is made between an original agreed 'capital', paid in by each partner, and shown more or less permanently as a separate item for each partner in the balance sheet, and profits subsequently earned *less* amounts withdrawn by the partners.[2] The ownership interest shown in the balance sheet thus remains divided over long periods into two main sections, 'capital' and 'profits not withdrawn', both sections being subdivided to show the separate interest of each partner. The subdivisions dealing with profits and drawings are often called *current accounts*. This distinction arises out of the

1 As we know the recorded values are not always good approximations of economic reality. This point, which must not be forgotten, means, among other things, that the capital shown in the balance sheet may be greater than, or less than, the capital as measured by market values.

2 The share of each partner in the total profit will be defined by the partnership agreement.

nature of the contract between the partners: if the partnership agreement requires each partner not to withdraw from the business any amount in excess of an agreed paid-in capital, the balance sheet must show how much of the ownership claim consists of this agreed capital. Thus the word 'capital' can mean the whole ownership interest, or only part of it, according to the context.

Capital and profit: limited companies

We now come to the accounting reports of limited companies, the most important form of business organization in this country.[1] The form of company accounting reports is largely governed by company law (as distinct from mutual agreement in the case of partners or personal views in the case of sole traders). Company balance sheets are required to show as a separate figure the amount of money paid in by the owners (the *members* or *shareholders*). This is called the share capital. All profits earned, less any payments out of these to the owners (which in companies are called, not drawings, but *dividends*) are shown separately: such retained profits are often called *reserves* or *surplus*. It is usual to include in the annual reports of companies a statement reconciling the part of the ownership interest represented by undistributed profit at the beginning of the year with the amount remaining undistributed at the end of the year, the difference being explained by the profit earned in the year (as shown by the profit and loss statement), *less* corporation tax payable on this profit, and *less* any dividends paid. This statement is the *appropriation account*. In published company reports it is usually printed immediately after the profit and loss statement and is often not distinguished clearly from it; but the analytical distinction is sharp and important: the profit and loss account shows the profit earned; the appropriation account shows how much of the profit has been withdrawn or

1 In legal theory a company is a fictitious 'person'; the business is owned by the company and the company is owned by the shareholders of the company. For reading on this see Gower, *Modern Company Law*. In the United States limited companies carrying on business are called 'business corporations'.

'appropriated' in the form of dividends paid to the shareholders, or as tax handed over to the Government.[1]

Finance from retained profit

The reader will notice that if the owner withdraws money from the business there is no economic criterion by which one can say whether he is withdrawing part of his original capital or part of any profit that has been earned; he is withdrawing an asset, and, as a result, the net ownership claim is reduced; the allocation of the reduction to the capital or to the profit part of the owner-ship interest is a matter of convention, though a convention which often has a legal basis.[2]

An important point to be noted at this stage is that profit earned is not the same as money received. The study of Tables 2.1, 2.2, and 3.1 should make it clear that profit is a measurement of the net increase in the recorded value of *all* the assets, *less* the liabilities, taken together. Hence a profit can arise in a period when the holding of money (cash) has *fallen*. This indeed has happened in our example. The final column of Table 2.2 shows that though the profit is £23, cash has fallen by £7. The net increase over the week in what is called *working capital*, that is, cash, trade debtors, stock, *less* trade creditors, all taken together, is only £13: this is £10 less than the profit. The difference is due to the withdrawal of £10 by the proprietor. Notice that leaving profit in the business is equivalent to providing extra ownership finance: the additional ownership claim finances the net increase in assets which gave rise to it. As soon as the profit arises the owner can be said to provide extra finance equal to that profit: he is from that time on exercising his right of choice not to withdraw from the business assets equivalent to the amount of the profit.[3]

1 Later the reader will learn, however, that border-line cases some-times arise in practice when it is difficult to decide if an item constitutes part of the profit calculation or an 'appropriation'.

2 Where companies are concerned the shareholders cannot, in general, legally withdraw *more* than the amount of the profit, and in the accounts dividends are always treated as withdrawals of profit.

3 In companies this right of choice is exercised by the directors of the company on behalf of the owners (the shareholders), sometimes whether they like it or not.

Comparison of sole trader, partnership and company balance sheets

Sole traders, partnerships, and companies differ, as we have said, in certain legal and economic respects. This, together with the conservatism of accountants, has led to some differences in the form of their balance sheets as these are usually presented to the owners. We shall illustrate the conventional forms used, so far as these relate to the ownership interest section, with some simple figures.

Let us imagine that we are considering the financial reports of a business for a particular calendar year 19—. The data are as follows:

	£
Money originally paid in by the owner was	800
Since then profits up to 1 January 19— have been	1,500
Money withdrawn up to 1 January 19— has been	1,300
Hence the sources of the ownership interest on 1 January 19— can be said to be:	
Original capital paid in	800
Profit earned and retained in the business	200
The ownership interest on 1 January 19— is	1,000
During the year 19— the profit, as shown by the profit and loss account, is, let us say	120
	1,120
The owner or owners withdraw from the business in 19—, say	80
The ownership interest on 31 December 19— is therefore	1,040

If these figures had related to the business of a sole trader, the normal form of the balance sheet would be like that shown in Table 3.2. Here the profit is merged each year with the rest of the ownership interest, drawings being deducted from the total; in such cases the reconciliation of the opening and closing figure of capital is usually shown in the balance sheet.

The balance sheet of the same business carried on by a company would be as in Table 3.3(A). Here share capital and undistributed profit are distinguished; this is a legal requirement. The presentation is simpler than in the case of the sole trader because in the case of companies it is the custom to present an appropriation account in which can be reconciled the figures of undistributed profit as at the beginning and end of the year. The appropriation account is shown in Table 3.3(B).

Partnership accounts are in this respect half-way between sole traders' accounts and company accounts. This is not surprising

TABLE 3.2

SOLE TRADER

Balance sheet at 31 December 19—

	£
Assets *less* liabilities[1]	1,040
Capital	
Balance at 1 January	1,000
add Profit for the year as shown in profit and loss account[2]	120
	1,120
less Drawings	80
Balance at 31 December	1,040

1 In practice the different assets and liabilities would be listed separately and in detail.

2 This figure would be explained in the separate profit and loss statement for the year.

when we remember that limited companies developed out of partnerships during the nineteenth century. Let us assume that the figures given above relate to a business in which there are two partners, X and Y, with equal shares in the original capital of £800, that the partners share profit equally, and that drawings have also been equally divided between them (i.e. have been in proportion to profit shares). We show the balance sheet, as it would probably be drawn up on the basis of the above figures, in Table 3.4(A). In such a case it is usual to present also an

TABLE 3.3

LIMITED COMPANY

(A)

Balance sheet at 31 December 19—

	£
Assets *less* liabilities[1]	1,040
Share capital[2]	800
Undistributed profit	240
	1,040

(B)

Appropriation account
for year to 31 December 19—

	£
Profit shown in profit and loss account	120
add Undistributed profit at 1 January	200
	320
less Dividends paid	80
Undistributed profit at 31 December	240

1 See footnote 1 to Table 3.2.

2 In a company the 'capital' is regarded as being divided into *shares* each of which carries a proportionate part of any benefits which the ownership claim may bring. The 'thing' that is subdivided in this way is really the total body of legal rights and duties of the owners, including the right to such dividends as are paid.

appropriation account showing the division of profit between partners.[3] This is shown in Table 3.4(B).

3 But not, as in companies, the partners' drawings; these are usually shown in the balance sheet.

TABLE 3.4

PARTNERSHIP

(A)

Balance sheet at 31 December 19—

	£	£	£
Assets *less* liabilities[1]			1,040

	X	Y	
Capital accounts	400	400	800
Current accounts			
Balance at 1 January	100	100	200
add Share of profit for year	60	60	120
	160	160	320
less Drawings	40	40	80
Balance at 31 December	120	120	240
			1,040

(B)

Appropriation account
for year to 31 December 19—

		£
Profit shown in profit and loss account		120
less Partners' shares X ½	60	
Y ½	60	
	—	120

1 See footnote 1 to Table 3.2.

It is usual to give in the balance sheet a detailed summary of
the changes in the partners' current accounts during the year, as
in Table 3.4(A). The partnership appropriation account shows
less than that of a company partly for historical reasons and
partly because there is an important difference of principle
between the current accounts of partners and the undistributed
profit of companies. Each partner's current account can, subject
to agreement, be altered separately by the partner in question
withdrawing money or, sometimes, paying money back into the
business (this is quite apart from changes in his agreed permanent

capital and any specific additional loans he may make to the business). Individual shareholders of companies, on the other hand, cannot withdraw their share of the profit earned by companies independently of other shareholders. All profit distributions are made on the same terms to all shareholders entitled, in proportion to the shares held.[1] Moreover, the dividend paid at any time may not legally exceed the amount of profit earned and not previously distributed.

1 There may, however, be different classes of shareholders, some of whom are given limited, but preferential, rights.

4

MANUFACTURING ACTIVITIES.
REVENUE AND EXPENSE ACCOUNTS

Transactions of a manufacturing business

We shall now analyse the transactions of a small manufacturing business carried on by a company. The data will again relate to a week's transactions, from one Saturday to the following Saturday. We shall assume that the business is run by a shareholder-manager.[1] There are two employees, one of whom is employed in the workshop and one in the office, and both the workshop and office are rented. The employees are paid weekly, on Friday. All money received is paid into the bank and all payments are made by cheque. We have:

Opening figures on the first Saturday night:

	£
Stocks:	
Tools	60
Raw materials	130
Work in progress	80
Finished goods	70
Trade debtors	40
Cash at bank	25
Trade creditors	30
Share capital	300
Undistributed profit	75

1 We shall assume for simplicity that the shareholder-manager is at present not being paid any remuneration. (Naturally he will have dividend expectations, however.)

Transactions:

Monday	a	Sold on credit, for £74, finished goods of balance sheet value £50.
Tuesday	b	Received £30 from trade debtors.
Wednesday	c	Paid £25 to trade creditors.
Thursday	d	Bought raw materials on credit at a cost of £20.
Friday	e	Recorded the fact that raw materials, of balance sheet value £47, had been used in production, thus reducing the value of raw material stock, with an equivalent increase in the value of work in progress.
	f	Recorded the fact that some of the tools had been partially worn out in production work. Value of the tools remaining estimated to be £55, implying a loss in value of £(60 − 55) = £5 during the week, this being regarded as causing an equivalent increase in value of the work in progress.
	g	Paid weekly wages, £26; half this amount, £13, representing the wage of the operative in the workshop, regarded as creating an equivalent increase in the value of work in progress.
	h	Paid weekly rent, £8; half of this, £4, the rent of the workshop, regarded as creating an equivalent increase in the value of work in progress.
	i	Recorded the fact that during the week part of the work in progress had been completed, the balance sheet value of this being £57.
Saturday		No transactions.

Transactions a, b and c are similar to those already discussed, except that the business is selling goods that it has manufactured instead of goods bought for resale. Transaction d is new: raw materials have been bought for manufacturing purposes. This transaction affects the balance sheet in the same way as the purchase of goods for resale, and the valuation conventions are similar: that is, the balance sheet value is the original cost of the material.

During the week, some of the raw materials are taken from store for production purposes (e). To record this we reduce the value of the asset *raw material* and increase, by the same amount, the asset *work in progress*. 'Work in progress' is the term used to describe partly manufactured products in any state of completion, from unworked raw material that has just been taken out of the store and placed on the production floor, to goods that have been completed but have not been finally transferred to the finished goods store or to the customer. The raw material figure in the balance sheet shows the value of the goods that should be in the raw material store, and the work in progress figure shows the value of the work that should be on the production floor: thus these figures can, among other things, be used as part of a system of control over valuable objects.

The work in progress value is the value placed on the raw material used for the work in question, plus a figure (calculated on a defined, conventional basis) for the cost of labour services and the services of other factors of production that have contributed to the work up to the date of the valuation.

It is assumed that the wages paid to the workshop operative measure the value added to the product by his work, and the amount of the wages is therefore added to the work in progress valuation (g). If, however, he only worked part of the time, e.g. because business was slack, but was paid for the whole week, only a proportion of his wages, appropriate to the work done, would be added to the value of work-in-progress; the rest would be treated, not as value added, but as an expense or loss in the same way as the wages of the office worker discussed below.

The services of the workshop contribute to the production. The workshop rent for the period is, therefore, also added to the value of the work in progress (h). Here, too, if the available time during the week is not wholly occupied in production, only a proportion may be added, the rest being treated as lost.

It is assumed that in the course of production some of the manufacturing tools have been physically used up, or have had their future usefulness reduced. The value thus used up is added to the balance sheet value of work in progress (f). The tools themselves will usually be valued at their original cost, and the loss in value (or *depreciation*) will be calculated as a proportion of this original cost. The value added to the work in progress in this respect is therefore usually part of the original cost of the tools. Here again only part of the depreciation may be added to the value of the work in progress if the tools have not been in normal use all the week.

During the week, the manufacture of a certain physical quantity of work in progress is completed and the balance sheet value of this, calculated by summing the components just described, is transferred to the classification *finished goods* (*i*). This implies that each time additional value is allotted to the work in progress it is allocated to a specific product or set of products: the £13 of wages cost added to work in progress for the week will, for example, be divided among the various jobs done on the basis of the time the workman has spent on each; the raw material cost will be allotted to the particular products for which the material is used; the depreciation of tools and the rent will be allocated in some convenient way, for example, on the basis of the time spent on each unit of output in the workshop, so that a job that has taken half the available working time in the week may have half the workshop rent added to its cost.[1]

The value of the finished goods calculated in this way is sometimes called the *manufacturing cost of production* or *works cost of production*. These terms are used to indicate that the balance sheet value has been calculated without taking into consideration the *administrative overhead costs* such as office wages and rent that are less closely concerned with the physical production activities than are the workshop expenses. Needless to say, the cost of production so calculated will only by accident be equal to the saleable value of the goods and in the general case will be less.

That part of the finished goods' value which consists of the material used in the product and the wages of the operatives directly concerned with making it is called the *prime cost* or *direct cost*.[2]

1 The purpose of such allocations (and their usefulness and significance) raise important economic questions that must be studied when the economic and management aspects of accounting are considered. Here we are concerned with the procedures.

2 Prime or direct cost may also include the cost of other services than labour where these are incurred for, and only for, a specific unit of product.

When the finished goods are sold the balance sheet values are adjusted in the same way as when part of a stock of goods originally bought for resale is sold (*a*). Like goods bought for resale, the manufactured goods are, as we have just seen, normally valued on the basis of original cost, though the calculation of this cost is more complicated than in the case of goods which are merely bought for resale without processing, and involves a greater number of arbitrary assumptions. In general the manufacturer will so plan that the average of this original cost, taken over the whole output, is below the sales value of the goods by a *gross profit margin* sufficient to meet the remaining expenses (here the office wages and rent), to remunerate the management, and to give an economic return on the capital value invested in the business.[1]

It is a matter of convention how much of the expenditure recorded in the accounts of a business in a given period is treated as a change in asset structure (as where a fall in cash is balanced by a rise in, say, work in progress) and how much is treated as an expense (as where a fall in cash is balanced by a fall in the ownership interest). As sales are made, so that the cash or debtors rise and the stock of finished goods falls, the net value of the balance sheet assets (*less* liabilities) rises by the excess of the sales value over the finished goods balance sheet valuation. In so far as amounts spent on rent, wages, etc., have been treated as an expense and *written off*, that is, removed from the balance sheet by a reduction in the ownership interest, the profit reported when the sale is finally recorded will be so much the greater, since the book value of the stock will be correspondingly lower. Different valuation methods may thus alter the distribution of profit reported as between different accounting periods. This is because a higher stock valuation in period 1 (i.e. the allocation of more rather than less expense to the work in progress value)

1 In the language of economic theory, management remuneration and a return on capital sufficient to make it worthwhile to continue the business are both 'costs'. Here practical and theoretical *language* (though not necessarily *ideas*) differ, for an accountant would not call any part of what he classifies as net profit, a 'cost'. (In our example management remuneration has to be met out of profit, though in the case of companies this usually takes the form of salaries that are a cost in the accounting sense.)

will raise the amount of the ownership interest at the end of period 1, but will reduce it by the same amount in the period in which the stock is sold, e.g. in period 2. (The longer the interval of time considered, however, the less will a change in the method of valuation of work in progress and finished goods at the beginning and end of the period affect the aggregate net profit reported during the interval, since these stock valuations will be an increasingly smaller proportion of the sales revenue as the period lengthens.[1]

Double entry analysis

We shall now summarize in double entry form the opening figures and the week's transactions given at the beginning of this chapter, using the kind of analysis that was employed in Table 2.3. This analysis is shown in Table 4.1. The reader should check the entries in this table against the original information.

Accounts (1), (2), (3), (4), (5) in Table 4.1 relate to assets. Accounts (7), (8), and (9) relate to claims on the business, (7) to

1 This discussion of stock valuation methods must be regarded as provisional. A number of important qualifications and amplifications, some of which we shall examine later, and some of which must be left for further reading, have necessarily been omitted at this stage. For example, the work in progress value is sometimes determined by summing only the raw materials and the wages of operatives directly concerned with production, all other expenses being treated 'as if' they were lost, and written off: stocks are valued 'at direct cost'. This obviously gives a lower value for work in progress and a correspondingly lower initial figure for profit than the method used in our example; but this is compensated for when the finished goods are sold, for the profit then shown is larger, *pro tanto*. Again, there are strong arguments for abandoning the original cost basis of valuation in favour of one based on current market prices in certain circumstances. The discussion of this is, however, outside the range of this book. Our main concern here is to understand the kind of procedures that are used in the construction of accounting reports. These procedures can be adapted to any method of valuation selected. The valuation methods we have described so far are in fact those which are most usual in practice. Evidently they must be known by anyone who wishes to understand accounting reports; but they are not necessarily the best, and the fact that they are described here does not imply that they are approved by the author as appropriate in all circumstances.

TABLE 4.1
DOUBLE ENTRY ANALYSIS

	(1) Tools		(2) Raw materials		(3) Work in progress		(4) Finished goods		(5) Trade debtors		(6) Cash at bank		(7) Trade creditors		(8) Share capital		(9) Profit and loss	
	Dr £	Cr £	Dr £	Cr £	Dr £	Cr £	Dr £	Cr £	Dr £	Cr £	Dr £	Cr £	Dr £	Cr £	Dr £	Cr £	Dr £	Cr £
Opening balances	60		130		80		70		40		25			30		300		75
Monday a								50	74									24
Tuesday b										30	30							
Wednesday c			20									25	25					
Thursday d				47	47									20				
Friday e		5			5													
f					13							26					13	
g					4							8					4	
h						57	57											
Totals	60	5	150	47	149	57	127	50	114	30	55	59	25	50	—	300	17	99
Closing balances	55		103		92		77		84		4		25		300		82

claims of creditors, and (8) and (9) to the ownership interest. The account in column (6), which shows transactions with the bank, is peculiar, in that for part of the period it records an asset and for part a liability. It will be noticed that when all the bank transactions are taken together there is a net excess of value on the credit side: cash payments are greater than the sum of the opening balance and receipts. This means that the business owes money to the bank at the end of the week: the bank has then a claim on the business. Thus the double entry rules allow an account which records an asset at one time to record a claim at another.

The balance sheets which would be obtained if the balances were extracted from Table 4.1 each day are shown in Table 4.2. The first line of Table 4.1 gives us the data for the opening balance sheet, shown in the first column of Table 4.2. The final line of Table 4.1 gives us the final column of Table 4.2. Each

TABLE 4.2

BALANCE SHEETS AT THE CLOSE OF BUSINESS

£

	Sat	Mon	Tues	Wed	Thurs	Fri	Sat
Tools	60	60	60	60	60	55	55
Raw materials	130	130	130	130	150	103	103
Work in progress	80	80	80	80	80	92	92
Finished goods	70	20	20	20	20	77	77
Trade debtors	40	114	84	84	84	84	84
Bank	25	25	55	30	30	—	—
Total assets	405	429	429	404	424	411	411
Trade creditors	30	30	30	5	25	25	25
Bank	—	—	—	—	—	4	4
Total liabilities	30	30	30	5	25	29	29
Share capital	300	300	300	300	300	300	300
Profit and loss	75	99	99	99	99	82	82
Total ownership interest	375	399	399	399	399	382	382
Total claims or finance	405	429	429	404	424	411	411

intervening column in Table 4.2 can be obtained in the same way by summing the columns of Table 4.1 down to the appropriate line and taking the difference between the total debits and total credits for each account.

The double entry analysis of Table 4.1 can also be used to derive a flow of funds statement. This is shown in Table 4.3. The figures in this can be checked from rows *a* to *i* in Table 4.1. (Remember that the + and − signs in the lower section of the flow of funds statement all relate to rises and falls in claims, themselves negative in the double entry scheme, and are therefore the opposite signs to those of the corresponding figures in the double entry accounts of Table 4.1.) The balance sheet for each day, as shown in Table 4.2, could, of course, have been built up from the balance sheet of the preceding day by applying the differences in Table 4.3.

TABLE 4.3

SOURCES AND USES OF FUNDS

£

	Sat–Mon	Mon–Tues	Tues–Wed	Wed–Thurs	Thurs–Fri	Fri–Sat	Week
Tools	—	—	—	—	− 5	—	− 5
Raw materials	—	—	—	+20	−47	—	−27
Work in progress	—	—	—	—	+12	—	+12
Finished goods	− 50	—	—	—	+57	—	+ 7
Trade debtors	+74	−30	—	—	—	—	+44
Bank	—	+30	−25	—	−34	—	−29[1]
Change in assets	+24	—	−25	+20	−17	—	+ 2
Trade creditors	—	—	−25	+20	—	—	− 5
Capital	—	—	—	—	—	—	—
Profit	+24	—	—	—	−17	—	+ 7
Change in claims	+24	—	−25	+20	−17	—	+ 2

[1] This net change over the week converts an asset of £25 on the first Saturday into a liability of £4 on the second Saturday: see Table 4.2.

These illustrations are not intended to show exactly how the figures in balance sheets are built up in practice: they are intended to bring out the relationships between the various kinds of accounting statement and to show in principle how transactions can be conveniently summarized and classified. Nevertheless the procedure just described does correspond with the normal accounting process in the sense that the accounting system must provide for the collection of the raw data (exemplified by the information given at the beginning of the chapter), for its assembly and analysis (exemplified by the classified summary in Table 4.1), and for its summary in accounting reports for the use of the management and others, of the type shown in Tables 4.2 and 4.3.

We can now proceed further by extracting a profit and loss report from the data in Column (9) of Table 4.1. The result is summarized, day by day, and for the whole week, in Section (A) of Table 4.4: here we have the revenue and expenses which are the components of the net profit earned. In Section (B) of Table 4.4 is the appropriation account, showing how the net profit of Section (A), added to the undistributed profit at the beginning of each day, gives the undistributed profit at the end of each day, while the last column gives similar information for the week as a whole. A line is provided for dividends paid to the owner (shareholder): in this example they happen to be zero, but if they existed they would reduce the ownership interest, though not, of course, as a business expense. Although it is often convenient for working purposes to merge Sections (A) and (B) (as was, for example, done in Column (9) of Table 4.1), the distinction between the two sections reflects, as already noted, an important economic difference, and should always be observed in the final accounting reports.

Revenue and expense accounts

The profit statement of Table 4.4 was obtained from the ledger account for profit and loss, Column (9) of Table 4.1. It was easy to analyse the items in this column into their appropriate classes because there were only a few transactions. In practice there are many transactions; therefore it is convenient to split up the profit and loss account and maintain a separate ledger account for each class of transaction for which a separate total is likely to be useful. The ledger accounts, it must be remembered, constitute the formal records that are built up from the various sources of original data, and from which accounting reports will be extracted as they are required.

Thus, instead of the single ledger account in Column (9) of Table 4.1, we could have three separate accounts for gross profit, wages, and rent, respectively, together with an additional account to show the effect of combining the three – that is, to summarize the information for presentation in Section (A) of Table 4.4. A fifth account could summarize the information of Section (B) of Table 4.4.

TABLE 4.4

(A) PROFIT AND LOSS STATEMENT

£

	Sat–Mon	Mon–Tues	Tues–Wed	Wed–Thurs	Thurs–Fri	Fri–Sat	Week
Revenue							
Gross profit	24	—	—	—	—	—	24
Expenses							
Rent	—	—	—	—	4	—	4
Wages	—	—	—	—	13	—	13
	—	—	—	—	17	—	17
Net profit	24	—	—	—	−17	—	7

(B) APPROPRIATION ACCOUNT

£

	Sat–Mon	Mon–Tues	Tues–Wed	Wed–Thurs	Thurs–Fri	Fri–Sat	Week
Net profit for period	24	—	—	—	−17	—	7
add Retained profit at beginning of period	75	99	99	99	99	82	75
	99	99	99	99	82	82	82
less Dividends	—	—	—	—	—	—	—
Retained profit at end of period[1]	99	99	99	99	82	82	82

1 The figures in this line tally with those shown in the 'profit' line of the balance sheet in Table 4.2. This table explains the figures in terms of specific business activities.

Table 4.5 shows how these ledger accounts would appear. The figures that appear in the various columns of that table all appeared in the profit column of Table 4.1, but each is now shown under its own classified heading (see items *a, g* and *h* in

Table 4.5). At the end of the period each column is totalled and the balance is entered. These balances are then transferred to the profit and loss column (see items *j*, *k* and *l*). This transfer (which can be regarded as a reclassification of part of the ownership interest) is made by cancelling the balance under the original classification – e.g. rent – by inserting an entry equal, but of opposite sign, to the existing balance, and making an entry of the same amount and sign as the existing balance in the new ledger account – e.g. profit and loss. Thus the rent debit balance of £4 is cancelled by a credit item of £4, and a new debit of £4 is entered in the profit and loss account.[1] When these entries have been made a balance is struck on the profit and loss account, giving the profit earned for the period, here £7.

The appropriation account in Column (14) shows as an opening balance the ownership claim for retained profit at the beginning of the period; the profit figure for the period is transferred to this account from the profit and loss account (item *m*); the closing balance is the sum of the two figures. The profit and loss and appropriation accounts thus correspond with the reports in Sections (A) and (B) of Table 4.4, and provide the information for these reports without further adjustment.

The analysis in Table 4.5 may seem to the reader repetitive, adding little or nothing to the information we already have. This is because we are dealing with a very simple example, and in particular with one in which each class of transaction is represented by one figure only. This is very far from being the case in real life. One must imagine the single items here shown in each of the columns headed 'gross profit', 'office wages', and 'office rent' replaced by a large number of figures, and the three columns themselves multiplied perhaps 100 or 1,000 times. The need for a detailed system of classification is then more apparent.

To sum up, Table 4.1, as extended by Table 4.5, represents, in summary form, the formal double entry system of the business; and Tables 4.2, 4.3 and 4.4 represent the periodic reports which are prepared from this system.

1 Remember that this rent is being treated as, in effect, a reduction in the ownership claim: the money has been spent – the owner can no longer claim it. This is shown as a debit – an offset against the ownership interest credit.

TABLE 4.5

EXTENSION OF DOUBLE ENTRY SUMMARY
(replacing Column (9) of Table 4.1)

	(10) Gross profit		(11) Office wages		(12) Office rent		(13) Profit and loss		(14) Appropriation	
	Dr £	Cr £	Dr £	Cr £	Dr £	Cr £	Dr £	Cr £	Dr £	Cr £
Opening balance	—	—	—	—	—	—	—	—	—	75
a Gross profit		24								
g Wages			13							
h Rent					4					
	—	24	13	—	4	—	—	—	—	75
Balances	—	24	13	—	4	—	—	—	—	75
j Transfer	24							24		
k "				13			13			
l "						4	4			
	24	24	13	13	4	4	17	24	—	75
Balances	—	—	—	—	—	—	—	7	—	75
m Transfer							7			7
							7	7	—	82
Closing balance	—	—	—	—	—	—	—	—	—	82

The above analysis shows how the various components of the profit section of the ownership claim can, when they are first recorded, be allotted to separate accounts in order to facilitate the analysis of the sources of profit and loss. They can then be reclassified to produce the profit and loss account. Finally the net profit for the period can be reclassified with the undistributed profit at the beginning of the period in the appropriation account.

Time lags in accounting records

A study of Table 4.4 suggests the need to consider the effect of time lags in making accounting entries. Balance sheet changes reflect both internal rearrangements of resources (such as a transfer from the raw material to the work in progress classification) and external transactions (such as the sale of goods to customers or purchases from suppliers). Both types of balance sheet change are usually recorded in the ledger accounts only at the end of given intervals. It is not normally practicable to keep all the accounting records adjusted continuously as economic circumstances change (though electronic computers are bringing us closer to being able to achieve this, where the cost is justified). For example, in a manufacturing business, raw materials may move into production throughout the week, but the fact may be entered in the formal accounting records as if the whole change occurred at the end of the working week (here Friday).[1] Similarly, the wages accruing to the labour force for work done throughout the week, and the corresponding increase imputed to the work in progress value, may not be recorded until the wages are paid at the end of the week.[2]

1 Though, of course, continuous subsidiary records will have to be maintained so that the information can be collected and summarized.

2 But if payment is made after the end of an accounting period – i.e. a period for which an accounting report is made – it is necessary to recognize in the balance sheet the amounts owing at that date: the dates of the accounting reports may therefore determine when such transactions are recorded.

LEDGER ACCOUNTS.
THE TRIAL BALANCE.
JOURNAL FORM.
CURRENT ASSETS

Ledger accounts

In previous chapters we set out the ledger accounts in columns in such a way that the correspondence between the debit and credit entries for each particular transaction could be easily seen and checked. Henceforth, however, we shall adopt a more flexible practice, writing down the accounts in any order and position that we find convenient. In this we shall be following business practice: any double entry system must consist of a set of ledger accounts, but the precise form they take, and their location, is a matter of choice.

We shall, for convenience, use here what is sometimes called the T account form (from the practice of ruling a line along the top of the account and another down the middle to divide the debit and credit sides, thus forming a kind of T). If we had set out the ledger accounts in Table 4.1 in this way, the cash account, for example, would have appeared as follows:

Cash at bank

	£		£
Balance	25	c	25
b	30	g	26
		h	8
	55		59
		Balance	4

This form is based on the traditional double entry ledger that was used in the Italian city states at least as early as the fourteenth century,[1] though some of the historical trimmings have been dropped.[2] It provides a convenient standard form for summarizing transactions, and for distinguishing clearly and quickly between debit and credit items when the logic of a particular transaction is being analysed.[3]

At this point an alternative way of recording balances in the traditional form of account should be noted. A purist could argue that to insert a balance in a ledger account as a new figure after ruling off the debit and credit columns is to violate the rule that every debit entry must be accompanied by a credit entry, since the new balance is only entered once. This objection is dealt with in traditional book-keeping by inserting the new balance twice, once on each side. Thus, in the cash account given above, the new balance of £4 is inserted on the credit side, as we have it, but the same figure is also inserted on the debit side (that is, on the side with the smaller total) above the ruling (so that it does not affect the new total). The total on the debit side

1 See Littleton and Yamey (mentioned on p. 27).
2 For example, the words 'to' and 'by' preceding debit and credit entries respectively, have been omitted.
3 An alternative form is often used, e.g. by accounting machines, in which an additional column allows the balance to be recorded after each transaction without entering totals, as follows:

Cash at bank

	Dr £	Cr £	Balance
Balance	25		25 dr
b	30		55 dr
c		25	30 dr
g		26	4 dr
h		8	4 cr

Here the balance column is not part of the double entry system, and can be omitted if desired. Note that it is necessary to indicate whether the figure in the balance column is a debit or a credit balance, since this is not indicated by its position, as in the T account.

above the ruling is then necessarily equal to the old total on the credit side, and our cash account appears as follows:

Cash at bank

	£		£
Balance (opening)[1]	25	*c*	25
b	30	*g*	26
Balance c/d	4	*h*	8
	—		—
	59		59
	═		═
		Balance b/d	4

The balance inserted above the ruling on the side with the smaller total is sometimes called the balance carried down (c/d for short) and the opening balance in the next period is called the balance brought down (b/d). The final result is just the same as before; but the accuracy of the new balance is proved visually by the equality of the preceding totals.

The set of T accounts needed to describe the transactions which were recorded in Tables 4.1 and 4.5 is given in Table 5.1. Readers are recommended to check the items from the former two tables into the accounts in Table 5.1, ticking off each figure in the old and in the new accounts as it is checked.

In Table 5.1 we have provided each item with a reference letter, as before; we have also inserted against each item the name of the account in which its contra, the opposite side of the double entry, appears. Thus item *d*, £20, on the debit side of raw materials account, is also referenced 'creditors', showing that the equivalent credit is in the trade creditors account; the latter is similarly referenced 'raw materials'. This is the traditional method of referencing in double entry book-keeping. In a good deal of practical book-keeping the only reference needed against an item in a double entry account is a code number or letter, and, if the date of the transaction is not implied by the reference number, a date, so that it is possible to trace each entry back to the original information from which it was derived. It is often

1 The original opening balance of £25 does not, in this case, have an entry of £25 offsetting it in the previous section of the cash account, as there was no previous period: the offsetting credit in this case is the credit balance found when all the balances on the other accounts shown on the first line of figures in Table 4.1, are summed.

useful, however, e.g. when analysing data in working papers for the preparation of accounting reports, to use the traditional method of referencing each debit or credit to its corresponding credit or debit, as we have done here.

TABLE 5.1

Tools

	£		£
Balance (opening)	60	f Work in progress	5
		Balance c/d	55
	60		60
Balance b/d	55		

Raw materials

	£		£
Balance (opening)	130	e Work in progress	47
d Creditors	20	Balance c/d	103
	150		150
Balance b/d	103		

Work in progress

	£		£
Balance (opening)	80	i Finished goods	57
e Raw materials	47	Balance c/d	92
f Tools	5		
g Bank	13		
h Bank	4		
	149		149
Balance b/d	92		

Finished goods

	£		£
Balance (opening)	70	a Debtors	50
i Work in progress	57	Balance c/d	77
	127		127
Balance b/d	77		

Trade debtors

	£		£
Balance (opening)	40	b Bank	30
a Finished goods and gross profit	74	Balance c/d	84
	114		114
Balance b/d	84		

Cash at bank

	£		£
Balance (opening)	25	c Creditors	25
b Debtors	30	g Work in progress and office wages	26
Balance c/d	4	h Work in progress and office rent	8
	59		59
		Balance b/d	4

Table 5.1 (continued)

Trade creditors

	£		£
c Bank	25	Balance (opening)	30
Balance c/d	25	d Raw materials	20
	50		50
		Balance b/d	25

Share capital

	£		£
		Balance (opening)	300

Gross profit

	£		£
Profit and loss	24	a Debtors	24

Office wages

	£		£
g Bank	13	k Profit and loss	13

Office rent

	£		£
h Bank	4	l Profit and loss	4

Profit and loss

	£		£
k Office wages	13	j Gross profit	24
l Office rent	4		
m Appropriation	7		
	24		24

Appropriation

	£		£
Balance c/d	82	Balance (opening)	75
		m Profit and loss	7
	82		82
		Balance b/d	82

The trial balance

On completion of a set of accounting entries it is often convenient, as a check on arithmetical accuracy, to make sure the
sums of the debit and the credit balances agree, by listing each

in a *trial balance* and comparing the totals. The trial balance for the above set of T accounts, proving the arithmetical accuracy of the work (subject to the existence of any compensating errors – errors of equal magnitude but opposite sign), is as follows:

	£	£
Tools	55	
Raw materials	103	
Work in progress	92	
Finished goods	77	
Trade debtors	84	
Cash at bank		4
Trade creditors		25
Capital		300
Appropriation		82
	411	411

Notice that in the trial balance, debit balances appear on the debit (left-hand) side and credit balances on the credit (right-hand) side as in the T ledger accounts. In this respect the trial balance differs from a formal balance sheet, which may be presented in any convenient way, but in Britain often has debits on the right-hand side and credits on the left-hand side.

Cost of sales

In practice it may be convenient to subdivide the ledger account that we have called 'gross profit'. The gross profit on a transaction is the resultant of two components, one debit – the cost of the goods sold (equal to the amount credited to the finished goods account), and one credit – the sales value (equal to the amount debited to the debtor or received in cash); the double entry for each such transaction was completed in the above example by crediting the gross profit as one item to a gross profit account. An alternative is to use two accounts, one called 'cost of goods sold' or 'cost of sales' and one called 'sales', in which the respective debits and credits are collected. This procedure is convenient if one wishes to analyse and study the sales figures by themselves, and to examine the relationship of the sales revenue to the cost of sales. It is, in fact, normal to show these two components separately in profit and loss reports to management and, increasingly, to shareholders. Their separation is also convenient from a book-keeping or data-processing point of view, in that the original data for the two components are in practice usually collected through quite different channels, the sales value information being derived from the section of the enterprise responsible for invoicing, and the cost of sales from the accounting section responsible for costing information.

Hence, we may replace the gross profit account in Table 5.1 by the following two accounts, the separate balances of which are both transferred to the profit and loss account:

	Cost of sales				*Sales*		
	£		£		£		£
a Finished goods	50	*n* Profit and loss	50	*p* Profit and loss	74	*a* Debtors	74

The profit and loss account then appears as follows:

	Profit and loss				
		£			£
n	Cost of sales	50	*p* Sales		74
k	Office wages	13			
l	Office rent	4			
m	Appropriation	7			
		74			74

The report derived from this account for presentation to management could run on these lines:

	£	£
Sales		74
less Cost of sales		50
Gross profit		24
less General expenses:		
Office rent	4	
Office wages	13	
		17
Net profit		7

The first three lines of this statement form what in older texts it has been customary to call the *trading account*.

Journal form

It is always necessary in practice to set up a systematic and carefully controlled procedure for collecting and classifying original data before it reaches the ledger accounts. We shall have more to say about this later. In earlier days it was customary to summarize the information for each transaction, showing the relevant debits and credits in chronological order in a book called the *journal*, which provided a link between the original information and the final ledger entries. The journal was not a formal part of the double entry; but all the double entry records were derived from it. In it the economic effect of each transaction was set out in a standard form which showed clearly the debits and credits concerned, and included a note or *narrative* explaining the transaction. The journal entry summarized, as it were, the accounting logic of each transaction.

The entry would take the following form:

			£	£
1823				
21 Jan.	J. Brown	dr	100	
	to Sales			100
	For sale of 20 bags of meal.			

This told the book-keeper to debit £100 to Brown's account and to credit £100 to the sales account; as he made the entries in the ledger he would note in the journal the pages in the ledger where these entries were to be found, and in the ledger the relevant page of the journal. Thus, the completion of the work of writing up the ledger, called *posting* the ledger, would be shown by the presence in the journal of all the ledger page references, and every entry in the ledger could be traced back to its source.

The journal is still used to some extent for unusual transactions that do not fit into the prescribed routines that have replaced it for most purposes. Our concern with it here, however, is with form: the journal form can provide a convenient shorthand description of any book-keeping entry, and is constantly used by accountants for this purpose (usually without the historical trimmings of 'dr' and 'to'). If an accountant writes:

	£	£
Interest on loan	100	
Cash		100

he is describing a transaction, the book-keeping results of which
will be to debit the interest account with £100 and to credit the
cash account with the same amount. The whole transaction is
thus summed up succinctly. Or suppose that only £60 is to be
paid out in cash to the lender immediately, the remaining £40
being paid later to the tax authorities on behalf of the lender,
as is required by law.[1] The tax authorities become creditors for
the £40. We show the whole transaction as follows:

	£	£
Interest on loan	100	
Cash		60
Inland Revenue Commissioners		40

Current assets

All the assets so far discussed have (with one exception) been
what are called *current assets*.[2] Broadly speaking, the category
covers the following: stocks of all kinds; trade debtors; cash, and
investments held temporarily as an alternative to cash; payments
in advance – the value of services which will be received after
the balance sheet date and which have already been paid for at
that date, such as insurance cover extending beyond the date of
the balance sheet: such services are valued by apportioning the
total cost over time on a straight-line basis, and taking the
proportion after the balance sheet date as the value at that date.
The general idea of current assets is that, if need arises, they
should be convertible into cash more easily, and with a smaller
sacrifice of value, than would be the case with other assets.

Market value of current assets

It has been stated above that for balance sheet purposes
accountants usually value stocks of all kinds on the basis of
some approximation – often involving an arbitrary choice of
assumptions – to their cost. This must now be qualified. When
the market value of stock has fallen to a point such that it

1 The proportion of the total interest payable to the tax authorities
depends upon the current standard rate of tax; our entry would be
correct if it were 40%.

2 The exception is the asset 'tools' in our example of a manufacturing business. This item is sometimes classified as current, but
not always.

appears that the ultimate selling value, after making a deduction for expenses of sale, is below the cost, the balance sheet value is reduced to the net realizable value. For this reason the normal valuation convention for stocks is known as the *cost or lower market value* rule. There is thus an asymmetry: rises in market value that occur before sale are ignored, but falls, if greater than a certain amount, are taken into consideration. This asymmetry is due to a traditional bias towards conservatism in accounting practice.

Sometimes the estimated current market replacement cost is taken as the maximum permissible balance sheet value, instead of the estimated net realizable value. This practice is still more conservative, since the replacement value will often be lower than the net resale value.

The cost or lower market value rule can be applied to a particular class of stock as a whole or to individual units. Suppose that the stock consisted of three items and that the data relating to these were:

	Cost	Market value
	£	£
X	10	7
Y	8	9
Z	14	11
	32	27

If the cost or lower market value rule were applied to the stock as a whole, the balance sheet valuation would be £27, this being below £32. In this case the increase in value of Y would partly offset the fall in value of X and Z. If, however, each item were considered separately we should have:

	Cost or lower market value
	£
X	7
Y	8
Z	11
	26

This gives a lower, and more conservative, valuation. Both methods are found in practice.

Where it becomes necessary to reduce the value of stock below its existing book value, there is an equivalent reduction in the profit. It would be reasonable to open a special account to which such losses could be debited, the balance on which at the end of the year would be transferred to the cost of sales account. If the total of such losses were shown in the profit and loss report as a separate part of the cost of sales, this would indicate the extent to which the business had in some sense incurred losses through failure to anticipate price changes or (where the fall in value was due to deterioration or obsolescence of stocks or errors in manufacture) through other kinds of failure. Often, however, such losses are merged in the cost of sales figure.

Whatever valuation convention is used in a given case, accountants lay great stress on the preservation of consistency in method from year to year. For although results will differ with the use of different conventions, and will therefore require different interpretations, changes in methods will introduce additional, arbitrary, effects. Sometimes there are reasons for changing the particular conventions employed; in such cases it is standard accounting practice to include in any profit and loss report a statement of the effect of the change on the figures. Thus, a change from an 'all in' to an 'item by item' interpretation of the cost or lower market value made at the end of a given year might well reduce the profit reported for the year. The profit and loss report should contain a statement drawing attention to the amount of the reduction so caused.

The valuation conventions applied to stock are, with qualifications, applied to other current assets. The general rule followed is that the value to be used is the value at the time the asset is acquired, less any amount needed to reduce that figure to its current realizable value. Thus, debts are included at the face value when the debt was created (e.g. by sale of goods), less an allowance for any expected loss in collection.[1]

1 It should be emphasized again that here we are only describing, in outline, the normal conventions. Many variants are found in practice, and alternative conventions have been advocated and in some cases introduced.

FIXED ASSETS.
LONG-TERM LIABILITIES.
DEPRECIATION

Analysis of transactions

We have now analysed the transactions of two different types of business. We have assumed, in order to keep the problem within bounds, that in one case the enterprise possesses only the type of asset we call 'current', and in the other case the business owns current assets and one class of the more permanent types of asset that are called 'fixed' (in this case, tools).[1] We have also assumed that all the liabilities are *current liabilities* – that is, they are short term, so that there are no long-term loans to the business.[2]

We shall now carry our study a step further by taking an example in which we assume that the main business asset is a fixed asset, and instead of all the longer-term finance being supplied by the owner, some is provided by an outside lender. For convenience we shall assume that the only current asset is cash at bank and that there are no current liabilities.

Let us assume that *A* carries on an owner-driver taxi business. His main asset is the taxi, which he buys partly out of money from his own pocket and partly by borrowing from a friend, *B*. His

---

1 Loose tools are, however, as noted above, sometimes classed as current because in some respects they are more like a stock of materials than a machine or a factory building.

2 Current liabilities are sometimes defined as those that must be settled within one year of their original creation. In practice, however, this rule is not followed rigidly.

only expenses are for fuel, oil, maintenance, garage, and licences. The summarized financial data for his first year are as follows:

Opening figures on the morning of 1 January:

	£
Cash at bank	1,000
Long-term loan from B	400
Capital supplied by A	600

Transactions (summarized for the year):

			£
1 Jan	a	Bought a taxi	950
1 Jan to 31 Dec	b	Received and paid into bank fares and tips	1,300
	c	Paid for licences, fuel, oil, repairs, and garage	603
	d	Paid 10% per annum interest on the loan	40
	e	Drew from the business bank account for personal expenses	500

A intends to sell the taxi and buy a new one at the end of 5 years. He expects the sale price to be £350. He therefore sets the average annual cost of using the taxi, i.e. its average annual fall in value or depreciation, at:

$$\frac{£(950-350)}{5}= \qquad 120[1]$$

No amounts are owing from or to A at the end of the year except for the loan from B. All payments are by cheque. We shall here, as throughout this work, ignore income tax and other tax. We shall assume that A wants his profits and drawings shown separately from his original capital.

For convenience we have in this example, unlike the previous ones, condensed the whole of each class of transactions for the period into a single figure. The table is therefore not chronological from a to f.

1 Compare this figure with the loss in value of the tools in the example at the beginning of Chapter 4.

First we carry out the double entry analysis. The ledger accounts recording and classifying the above information are shown in Table 6.1. The entries in these include the closing of the revenue and expense accounts, that is the transfer of the various revenue and expense balances to the profit and loss

TABLE 6.1

Capital

		£
	Balance (opening)	600

Loan (B)

		£
	Balance (opening)	400

Cash at bank

	£		£
Balance (opening)	1,000	a Taxi	950
b Fares	1,300	c Running expenses	603
		d Interest	40
		e Current	500
		Balance c/d	207
	2,300		2,300
Balance b/d	207		

Taxi

	£		£
a Cash	950	f Depreciation	120
		Balance c/d	830
	950		950
Balance b/d	830		

Revenue from fares

	£		£
g Profit and loss	1,300	b Cash	1,300

Running expenses

	£		£
c Cash	603	h Profit and loss	603

Loan interest

	£		£
d Cash	40	i Profit and loss	40

Depreciation

	£		£
f Taxi	120	j Profit and loss	120

Profit and loss

	£		£
h Running expenses	603	g Fares	1,300
i Loan interest	40		
j Depreciation	120		
k Current account	537		
	1,300		1,300

Current account

	£		£
e Cash	500	k Profit and loss	537
Balance c/d	37		
	537		537
		Balance b/d	37

account, and the transfer in turn of the balance of net profit to the current account (the name sometimes given to the sole trader's appropriation account when profit and drawings are not transferred directly to the capital account).

The opening and closing balance sheets are given in Table 6.2. The reader should check that the figures in these correspond respectively to the opening and closing balances in the ledger accounts of Table 6.1.

TABLE 6.2

BALANCE SHEETS

	1 January £	31 December £
Taxi	—	830
Cash at bank	1,000	207
Total assets	1,000	1,037
Loan from *B*	400	400
Capital	600	600
Profit	—	37
	600	637
Total finance	1,000	1,037

The profit and loss report for the owner can be extracted from the double entry profit and loss account. We have:

	£	£
Revenue from fares		1,300
less Running expenses	603	
Interest	40	
Depreciation	120	
	—	763
Net profit for year		537

The difference between this net profit and the drawings is the net profit retained (or 'carried forward') in the business, as shown by the current (or appropriation) account:

	£
Net profit for year, as above	537
less Drawings	500
Profit carried forward	37

In the conventional accounting report of a sole trader's business the net profit and the drawings may, as noted earlier, be merged in the figure of capital, so that no distinction is made in the closing balance sheet between the original paid-in capital and the retained profit. We should then have:

	£
Capital, 1 January	600
Net profit for year as shown in profit and loss statement	537
	1,137
less Drawings	500
Capital, 31 December	637

A flow of funds statement for the year would appear as follows:

	£
Taxi	+830
Cash at bank	−793
	+ 37
Profit *less* drawings	+ 37

The rise in value under the heading 'taxi' is the net result of two items, an initial cash expenditure of £950 and an estimated subsequent loss in value (depreciation) of £120.

An alternative and perhaps more significant way of presenting the flow of funds statement would be as follows:

	£
Finance provided during year:	
Cash flow from operations	
Amount representing recovery of depreciation	120
Amount representing net profit	537
	657
Reduction in initial cash balance	793
	1,450
Finance used during year:	
Expenditure on new taxi	950
Drawings	500
	1,450

This brings out clearly that the cash inflow from operations was greater than the net profit by the amount estimated for the depreciation of the taxi during the year.

Depreciation

We shall now consider the economic significance of the depreciation figure. In the above example, the profit retained at the end of the year is £37. The cash balance at that date is £207. Suppose that the remaining £37 of the year's profit is withdrawn on 31 December: we are still left with £170 of cash at the bank.

The balance sheet now reads:

	£
Taxi	830
Cash	170
Total assets	1,000
Loan	400
Capital	600
Profit	—
	600
Total finance	1,000

The original cash brought into the business was £1,000. Of this, £950 was spent on the taxi, leaving £50. This £50 has now grown to £170. The increase of £120 in cash is equal in amount to that part of the year's expenses (as shown in the profit and loss report above) not spent in cash, that is, to the depreciation: this is the estimated amount of the fall in value of a fixed asset, the taxi. This is not a current *cash* expense; but we have, so to speak, 'spent' £120 of the taxi's value.

Let us continue the story for the next four years, on the assumption that each year is a replica of the first and that the proprietor withdraws from the business all his net profits as now shown in the accounts. At the end of the fifth year the balance sheet is as follows:

	£
Taxi	350
This has been reduced (written down) by £120 each year for 5 years ($950 - 5 \times 120 = 350$)	
Cash	650
This has grown by £120 each year ($1,000 - 950 + 5 \times 120 = 650$)	
	1,000
Loan (unchanged)	400
Capital (unchanged, all profit having been withdrawn)	600
	1,000

On the morning of the next day, 1 January of the sixth year, the old taxi is sold for the expected £350. We have then:

	£
Taxi ($350 - 350$)	—
Cash ($650 + 350$)	1,000
	1,000
Loan	400
Capital	600
	1,000

We have thus reached the same position as that at which we started, five years ago, and the cycle can begin again.

This demonstrates the nature of the depreciation calculation and its relation to profit determination. It shows that the reported annual level of profit will depend, among other things, upon the convention of depreciation measurement adopted and the assumptions made about the life and ultimate value of the asset.[1]

Suppose that depreciation of the taxi had been ignored when the profit was calculated. The profit would then be reported as £657 (£537 + £120). Suppose this amount was withdrawn from the business each year. At the end of the five years there would not be assets of sufficient value to buy a new taxi (or, if the business was not to be continued, to repay the loan and withdraw all the original capital). The balance sheet would tell exactly the same story at the end of the first and of each following year, namely:

	£
Taxi	950
Cash	50
	1,000
Loan	400
Capital	600
	1,000

When the taxi was sold at the end of the fifth year, £350 of its balance sheet value would be converted into cash, leaving £600 of apparent value in the balance sheet thus:

	£
Taxi (950 − 350)	600
Cash	400
	1,000
Loan	400
Capital	600
	1,000

1 The total depreciation in the five years is £600. This was spread on a straight-line or linear basis, i.e. at a steady rate of £120 per annum. Other ways of spreading this £600 over the period may be used; we shall not discuss these here, however.

But the taxi would have gone and it is clear that the £600 would not correspond, even roughly, to reality. We should have to record a 'book loss' of £600. ('Book' because the real economic loss was incurred earlier: the taxi loses value throughout its life and we are only recognizing belatedly an economic event that has already happened.) The ownership claim is consequently not worth £600 or anything in the neighbourhood of that sum. It is indeed zero. We have, when the balance sheet is adjusted, to show this fact:

		£
Taxi (600 − 600)		—
Cash		400
		400
Loan		400
Capital	600	
less Loss	600	
	—	—
		400

As it happens, the figures we have chosen are such that in this case there would have been just enough cash left to repay the loan; but this is accidental. In other words, by failing to record the steady fall in value of an asset, *A* could have deceived himself (or others, such as *B*, whose loan is in jeopardy) as to his economic situation.

In a sole trader's business (or partnership business, if the partners so agree) there is, in fact, nothing to prevent an owner from withdrawing from the business a greater sum than the net profit earned, although if he does so he may have to pay money into the business again later if he wishes to carry on, or meet his obligations. The withdrawal of cash may indeed sometimes represent the best use which an owner can make of the surplus cash which has built up, e.g. before the time comes for the replacement of the fixed assets. For the time being he may be able to earn more by using the money outside the business than within; or he may prefer to use it for personal needs. But this does not affect the principles of profit measurement. Suppose that A had shown in his balance sheet the loss in value of his taxi, but had still withdrawn for personal use an annual cash sum of £657. Compare the balance sheet at the end of the first year with that in which no depreciation calculation was made:

	I No depreciation		II With depreciation	
	£		£	£
Taxi	950	Taxi:		
Cash	50	Cost	950	
		less Depreciation	120	
				830
		Cash		50
	1,000			880
Loan	400	Loan		400
Capital	600	Capital	600	
		less Drawings	120	
				480
	1,000			880

The cash is the same in both cases; but while I shows the taxi at its original cost, and suggests that the ownership claim is still £600, II shows the depreciated value of the taxi and indicates clearly that A has taken out of the business not only all the profit but also some of his original invested capital. Tables 6.3 and 6.4 show the changes in the balance sheets through the five years on the two assumptions. Note that while in both cases the balance sheets show the assets to be worth £1,000 in total after distribution of profit throughout the period, this is only a true statement for assumption II.

We must not suggest that the depreciation *provision*, as it is usually called, is a very precise measurement of the loss in value of an asset. In practice its estimation and interpretation are fraught with difficulties. This, however, is well known. To omit depreciation altogether would be to suggest that no economic change had occurred with respect to the asset concerned. A reasonable approximation, based on known assumptions, is usually better than no information at all.

TABLE 6.3

BALANCE SHEETS ON ASSUMPTION THAT NO DEPRECIATION IS CHARGED AND DISTRIBUTIONS ARE EQUAL TO PROFIT REPORTED (ASSUMPTION 1)

£

	1 Jan	Year 1 31 Dec a	b	Year 2 31 Dec a	b	...	Year 5 31 Dec a	b	Year 6 1 Jan
Taxi	—	950	950	950	950	...	950	950	—
Cash	1,000	707	50	707	50	...	707	50	400
	1,000	1,657	1,000	1,657	1,000	...	1,657	1,000	400
Loan	400	400	400	400	400	...	400	400	400
Capital	600	600	600	600	600	...	600	600	600
Profit	—	657	—	657	—	...	657	—	−600 (loss)
	1,000	1,657	1,000	1,657	1,000	...	1,657	1,000	400

a = before profit distributed for year
b = after   "   "   "   "

TABLE 6.4

BALANCE SHEETS ON ASSUMPTION THAT STRAIGHT-LINE DEPRECIATION IS CHARGED AND DISTRIBUTIONS ARE EQUAL TO PROFIT REPORTED (ASSUMPTION II)

£

	1 Jan	Year 1 31 Dec		Year 2 31 Dec		...	Year 5 31 Dec		Year 6 1 Jan
		a	b	a	b		a	b	
Taxi	—	830	830	710	710	...	350	350	—
Cash	1,000	707	170	827	290	...	1,187	650	1,000
	1,000	1,537	1,000	1,537	1,000		1,537	1,000	1,000
Loan	400	400	400	400	400	...	400	400	400
Capital	600	600	600	600	600		600	600	600
Profit	—	537	—	537	—		537	—	—
	1,000	1,537	1,000	1,537	1,000	...	1,537	1,000	1,000

a = before profit distributed for year
b = after   „   „   „   „

It should be noted that in practice the single asset 'cash' that we have shown in this simplified example would be represented by a set of current assets and liabilities, and the taxi by a collection of different fixed assets.

Although what follows is not directly relevant to depreciation or profit measurement, it should be noted (since the example we have used may otherwise mislead) that it would usually be a waste of resources from the business owner's point of view to accumulate in the business a cash balance that would not be required for the replacement of assets for some years; it would be normal to use the available cash in the interval to expand the earning power of the business, for example by acquiring additional stock in trade or fixed assets, or both, or possibly by investing in other businesses. When the time came for the replacement of fixed assets the fact that the business had expanded and presumably become more profitable (and therefore more valuable) would make it correspondingly easier to raise additional finance from outside, e.g. in the form of an additional loan, the interest on which could be met out of the cash flow arising from the additional profit. There are many other financing possibilities, such as the use for the repayment of loans of funds not needed for the time being, with the intention of borrowing again when finance is needed for replacement or expansion at some later date.

Cash flow

The term 'cash expenses' may be used to distinguish from depreciation the expenses that will involve a cash outlay at once or fairly soon. The adjective 'cash' may thus be used in a special sense to describe expenses represented by falls in current assets or rises in current liabilities, both of which affect the short run liquidity of the business. The difference between revenue and cash expenses is sometimes called the *cash flow*. In general, the annual reduction in the value of fixed assets which we call depreciation has no short run effect on the business liquidity; hence the failure to make, and record, a reasonable estimate of depreciation may not become apparent for a relatively long period, during which shareholders and other owners, and long-term creditors, may be deceived about both the long run profitability of the business and the current values of its fixed assets.[1]

Price level changes

The economic picture presented by a balance sheet nearly always deviates to a greater or lesser extent from that which would be given by an up to date assessment of asset values. This is largely due to the fact that it is impossible to forecast with certainty what the future (on which the value to an enterprise of most of its assets depends) holds; though it may be argued that this excuse is sometimes pressed too far. It follows that the profit figure (which is the algebraic sum of certain of the changes in balance sheet values over a given period) gives a correspondingly poorer reflection of economic reality.

A special, and sometimes serious, error arises when there have been changes in the general level of prices. When based on original cost, the balance sheet values of the assets that are not of fixed money value (such assets as stocks, and plant and equipment) may deviate widely from their current economic values; and profit and loss debits for depreciation and for cost of sales calculated on the basis of the original cost may cease to indicate at all satisfactorily the current economic cost of holding and using the assets over a given period; net profit is correspondingly distorted. The simplest and most obvious remedy is to revalue the assets as best one can and calculate the annual costs on the basis of the adjusted values. In recent years it has become increasingly (though not yet generally) accepted that such adjustments should be made. There is no difficulty in accommodating them within the double entry system; the main difficulties arise out of the problem of selecting a suitable price index number or other criterion for revaluation. The subject will, therefore, be left for later study, and (since this book is not concerned primarily with valuation questions) will not be discussed further here.

1 It is true that the balance sheet values of fixed assets are seldom very good indicators of their current economic value. But the omission of depreciation will, in general, make them even worse indicators. This is still more true of the profit and loss account, which measures *changes* in values.

PROBLEMS IN DOUBLE ENTRY
AND FINAL ACCOUNTS

Introduction

The essential principles have now been covered. In this chapter
we shall work through a number of examples to illustrate
applications of these principles. The reader should work through
each example carefully. He should tick off each item in the list
of data given as he notes how they are entered in the accounts;
at the same time he should tick the relevant item in the solution.
Similarly he should note how the totals and balances are obtained
in the solution, and should check the transfers between accounts,
again ticking each debit against its corresponding credit. Finally
he should check the figures in the 'final accounts' – the accounting reports in the form of profit and loss accounts, balance sheets,
and so on – against the double entry records from which they
are obtained. It is good practice to work out the exercise for
oneself before looking at the solution.

In the solutions to some of the examples the double entry
analysis given represents what would be in practice the formal
records of the relevant business; in others it is the working
method by which a particular report or estimate is obtained, the
problem being such that the business's formal accounting system
would not be affected.

Example 1

Record the following transactions, relating to the business of a
trader, X, in double entry form, using schematic T accounts.

Jan 1   *a* *X* starts the business by paying £600 from his private funds into the business bank account.

6   *b* Wages paid by drawing cash from bank, £20.

6   *c* Fittings (to be treated as fixed assets) bought and paid for by cheque, £32.

8   *d* Goods for stock bought from *S* Ltd. on credit, £516.

10   *e* Goods sold to *Z* on credit, £206. (Note: as we are not told the cost of sales, this has to be worked out – see *l* below.)

12   *f* *S* Ltd. are paid in full by cheque.

13   *g* Goods are sold for cash, which is paid into the bank, £116.

14   *h* One month's rent is paid, by cheque, £40.

19   *i* *Z* pays in full. The money is paid into the bank.

20   *j* Goods are sold to *Y* on credit, £86.

31   *k* The business's debt for electricity supplied during the month is recorded, £5.

    l The stock remaining is valued at £311. The difference between this and the stock bought is recorded as cost of sales.

    m The month's depreciation of fittings is estimated as 10% of cost.

Prove the accuracy of your work by listing, in debit and credit columns, the balances on the ledger accounts, that is, by drawing up a trial balance as at the end of January. You are not asked to prepare a profit and loss account or a balance sheet.

The solution of this problem is given below. The cost of sales is found by subtracting the closing stock valuation of £311 from the amount of stock bought during the month, £516. The £311 is then the closing balance of stock. In businesses in which no continuous stock record is kept the cost of sales can only be found in this way.

The depreciation of fittings is 10% of £32, that is, £3 to the nearest £. In the solution we show the balance of the fittings account as reduced by this amount. It is often convenient, however, to use a second account in which the amount of depreciation to be deducted from an asset (the depreciation provision) is accumulated as a credit balance, a kind of negative asset, so that the net balance sheet value of the asset is obtained as the difference between the debit balance on the asset account and the credit balance on the depreciation provision account. (The latter is to be distinguished from the account that shows the debit for the depreciation expense which will be transferred to the profit and loss account.)

Note that in this example we are recording individual debtors and creditors as distinct from the totals of trade debtors and trade creditors in previous examples. In small businesses it may be possible to dispense with total accounts. In most businesses, however, there are so many debtors and creditors that it is essential to use them. We shall discuss in Chapter 8 how the record of individual debts and liabilities is linked up with the total accounts.

Bank

	£		£
a Capital	600	b Wages	20
g Sales	116	c Fittings	32
i Z	206	f S Ltd.	516
		h Rent	40
		Balance c/d	314
	922		922
Balance b/d	314		

Capital

	£		£
		a Bank	600

Wages

	£		£
b Bank	20		

Fittings

	£		£
c Bank	32	m Depreciation	3
		Balance c/d	29
	32		32
Balance b/d	29		

Stock

	£		£
d S Ltd.	516	l Cost of sales	205
		Balance c/d	311
	516		516
Balance b/d	311		

S Ltd.

	£		£
Bank	516	d Stock	516

	Sales				*Z*		
		£			£		£
	e Z	206		e Sales	206	i Bank	206
	g Bank	116					
	j Y	86					
		408					

	Rent			*Y*	
		£			£
h Bank		40	j Sales		86

	Electricity			*Electricity Board*	
		£			£
k El. Bd.		5		k Electricity	5

	Cost of sales			*Depreciation (expense)*	
		£			£
l Stock		205	m Fittings		3

Trial Balance, 31 January

	£	£
Bank	314	
Capital		600
Wages	20	
Fittings	29	
Stock	311	
Sales		408
Rent	40	
Y (debtor)	86	
Electricity	5	
Electricity Board (creditor)		5
Cost of sales	205	
Depreciation (expense)	3	
	1,013	1,013

Example 2

Use the results of Example 1.

Transfer the balances on the sales and cost of sales accounts to a trading account, and obtain the gross profit as a balance.

Transfer the gross profit, and the balances on the expense accounts, to a profit and loss account, and obtain the net profit as a balance.

Transfer the net profit to the capital account.

Prepare a new trial balance.

Using the figures in the relevant ledger accounts draft a trading and a profit and loss account and a balance sheet as at 31 January, in a form suitable for report to the owner.

In this example we have distinguished between the *trading account* (showing sales, cost of sales and, as a balance, gross profit) and the *profit and loss account*. This distinction is now tending to become obsolete; what is here distinguished as the trading account is just as likely to be merged in the profit and loss account. However, the old form is still used a good deal. The solution follows; only the accounts that are changed are shown; the others remain as in the solution of Example 1.

First we have the double entry accounts:

Trading account

	£		£
Cost of sales	205	Sales	408
Gross profit trans-ferred	203		
	408		408

Profit and loss account

	£		£
Rent	40	Gross profit trans-ferred	203
Wages	20		
Electricity	5		
Depreciation	3		
Balance c/d	135		
	203		203
Net profit transferred to Capital	135	Balance b/d	135

Capital

	£		£
Balance c/d	735	Balance b/d	600
		Profit and loss	135
	735		735
		Balance b/d	735

Sales

	£		£
Trading a/c	408	Balance b/d	408

Cost of sales

	£		£
Balance b/d	205	Trading a/c	205

Rent

	£		£
Balance b/d	40	Profit and loss	40

Wages				Electricity			
	£		£		£		£
Balance b/d	20	Profit and loss	20	Balance b/d	5	Profit and loss	5

Depreciation (expense)

	£		£
Balance b/d	3	Profit and loss	3

Trial balance, 31 January (after closing entries)

		£	£
Capital			735
Bank	(as in Example 1)	314	
Fittings	,, ,, ,, ,,	29	
Stock	,, ,, ,, ,,	311	
Debtor (Y)	,, ,, ,, ,,	86	
Creditor (Electricity Board)	,, ,, ,, ,,		5
		740	740

The reports to the owner are as follows:

Trading and profit and loss account
January 19—

	£	£
Sales		408
less Cost of sales		205
Gross profit		203
less Rent	40	
Wages	20	
Electricity	5	
Depreciation	3	
		68
Net profit		135

Balance sheet, 31 January 19—

	£	£
Fittings at cost *less* depreciation		29
Stock	311	
Trade debtor	86	
Cash at bank	314	
	——	711
		740
Capital		
Balance 1 January	600	
Profit for January	135	
	——	735
Creditor for expenses		5
		740

The form of these final accounts, and of those given in the following examples, should be noted. In particular note the division of the assets in the balance sheet into the two groups of fixed and current assets, and the order in which the assets are listed. It is usual when drafting a balance sheet to 'marshal' assets in either decreasing or increasing order of liquidity, so that the most liquid, cash, comes last (or first). In fact it is not always easy to say whether one asset is more liquid than another. There has developed, however, a fairly standard conventional 'order of liquidity' which we shall follow here: it is convenient to follow standard practice in this respect, as this makes accounting reports easier to read.

Similarly, current liabilities (those due for payment within about a year) are grouped separately from others, and there is a tendency to list the liabilities in the order in which they are due for payment.

Example 3

From the following trial balance as at 31 March 1962, taken from the ledger of *A*, a trader, prepare final accounts for the financial year to 31 March 1962:

	£	£
Capital, 1 April 1961		1,600
Sales		5,900
Cost of sales	3,220	
Stock, 31 March 1962	510	
Rent	100	
Returns inward	160	
Cash discounts allowed	150	
Cash discounts received		190
Drawings	581	
Furniture and fittings at cost	580	
Depreciation (provision)		160
,, (expense)	29	
Bank	240	
Salaries	1,100	
General expenses, including lighting and heating, insurance, postage, and telephone	180	
Debtors	2,300	
Creditors		1,300
	9,150	9,150

Certain of the terms given above are new. Their meanings are as follows:

(1) Returns inward: this debit is to be treated as a reduction in the sales; it represents the cancellation of certain sales by return of the goods. (The closing stock given must be assumed to include the goods sent back.)

(2) Discounts allowed: this debit is the counterpart of a credit or credits to debtors accounts. A percentage allowance is often made to a debtor if he pays before the end of a given time period and his account is credited with this. The corresponding debit represents a financial expense.[1]

(3) Discounts received: here it is the creditors whose claims have been reduced for a similar reason. The credit is, therefore, a financial gain.

(4) Depreciation provision: this was explained in Example 1. It is really an offset to the corresponding asset account.

1 Earlier payment of debts may save interest on a bank overdraft; in any case it gives the enterprise additional finance.

The ledger accounts will be as follows:

Capital

	£		£
Drawings	581	Balance	
Balance		b/d	1,600
c/d	2,170	Profit and	
		loss	1,151
	2,751		2,751
		Balance	
		b/d	2,170

Sales

	£		£
Profit and		Balance	
loss	5,900	b/d	5,900

Cost of sales

	£		£
Balance		Profit and	
b/d	3,220	loss	3,220

Stock

	£		
Balance b/d	510		

Rent

	£		£
Balance b/d	100	Profit and	
		loss	100

Returns inward

	£		£
Balance b/d	160	Profit and	
		loss	160

Cash discounts allowed

	£		£
Balance b/d	150	Profit and	
		loss	150

Cash discounts received

	£		£
Profit and		Balance b/d	190
loss	190		

Drawings

	£		£
Balance b/d	581	Capital	581

Furniture and fittings

	£		
Balance b/d	580		

Depreciation provision

		£
	Balance b/d	160

Depreciation (expense)

	£		£
Balance b/d	29	Profit and	
		loss	29

Bank

	£		
Balance b/d	240		

Salaries

	£		£
Balance		Profit and	
b/d	1,100	loss	1,100

4

General expenses			Debtors		
	£	£		£	
Balance b/d 180	Profit and loss	180	Balance b/d	2,300	

Creditors

	£
Balance b/d	1,300

Trading and profit and loss account

	£		£
Returns[1]	160	Sales	5,900
Cost of sales	3,220	Discounts	
Rent	100	received	190
Salaries	1,100		
General expenses	180		
Depreciation	29		
Discounts allowed	150		
Balance, net profit transferred to capital	1,151		
	6,090		6,090

Final trial balance

	£	£
Capital		2,170
Stock	510	
Furniture and fittings	580	
Depreciation		160
Bank	240	
Debtors	2,300	
Creditors		1,300
	3,630	3,630

The reports can now be drafted, and will appear as set out below.

In this example we have shown all the ledger accounts in order to give the reader a complete picture. If the problem was merely to prepare accounting reports (as distinct from showing the ledger entries too) it is clear that we could have worked directly

1 In the report this figure will be deducted from sales.

from the original trial balance, copying out only such ledger accounts as were needed to check any adjustments to be made to the figures: in this particular example we could have prepared the final accounting reports directly from the original data.

Until, however, one has the confidence that goes with complete understanding and a good deal of practice, it is probably better to write down the ledger accounts as a first step in the solution, since this, though slower, takes one back to first principles.

In the report, the final balance of the capital, £2,170, could have been inserted in the balance sheet without further detail, the reconciliation of the figure with the opening balance, the profit, and the drawings being relegated to a separate statement. Here the more usual practice is followed.

There is a good deal to be said for the 'narrative' or 'columnar' form of presentation for accounting reports used below: it is usually easier for laymen to understand, and it facilitates the comparison of the results of successive periods. On the other hand, the T form sometimes economizes space; and is probably quicker to read if one understands accounts.

A

Trading and profit and loss account
Year to 31 March 1962

		£	£
Sales *less* returns			5,740
less Cost of sales			3,220
Gross profit			2,520
Discounts received			190
			2,710
less Rent		100	
Salaries		1,100	
Lighting, heating, insurance, postage, and sundries		180	
Depreciation		29	
Discounts allowed		150	
		——	1,559
Net profit for year as shown in balance sheet			1,151

Balance sheet as at 31 March 1962

		£
Fixed asset		
Furniture and fittings at cost		580
less Depreciation		160
		420
Current assets		
Stock	510	
Debtors	2,300	
Cash at bank	240	
	3,050	
less Current liabilities		
Creditors	1,300	
		1,750
Net assets		2,170
Represented by capital		
Balance at 1 April 1961		1,600
Profit for year to 31 March 1962		1,151
		2,751
less Drawings for year to 31 March 1962		581
Balance at 31 March 1962		2,170

Example 4

The trial balance below has been taken from the books of *AB*, a wholesale trader. From this trial balance prepare final accounts (trading and profit and loss account and balance sheet) for the year to 31 December, in a form suitable for presentation to the management, taking into account the additional information provided.

Trial balance
31 December

	£	£
Stock	1,700	
Sales		10,932
Trade debtors	1,124	
Trade creditors		782
Furniture and equipment (original cost)	1,560	
Depreciation provision		496
Returns	62	
Salaries	1,300	
Bad debts provision		24
General expenses	948	
Cost of sales	7,063	
Cash at bank	362	
Cash in hand (petty cash)	25	
Drawings	510	
Capital (as at 1 January		2,420
	14,654	14,654

At the end of the year the following matters had not been recorded in the books:

(a) Salaries accrued due but unpaid amounted to £15.

(b) Depreciation on furniture and equipment for the year is to be at the rate of 10% per annum on original cost

(c) The trade debtors' balance included £24 considered irrecoverable.

(d) A general bad debts provision is to be made, equal to 5% of the debtors' balance in the balance sheet before deduction of the general provision.

Before we tackle the problem, some explanation is necessary of items (c) and (d) above. When a debt becomes irrecoverable or finally 'bad' it is 'written off as a bad debt'. This means that the total of the debtors is reduced by a credit entry equal to the amount lost, and a corresponding debit is made to an expense account called *bad debts*, or sometimes *bad and doubtful debts*.

Sometimes when a debt or part of a debt is of doubtful value, but not finally known to be bad, the total of debtors is not reduced (which means that the amount written off will be lost sight of), but instead the amount that is doubtful is credited to a *bad debts provision account*, as, in effect, a negative asset; this is shown in the balance sheet as a deduction from debtors; the corresponding debit entry again is made in the bad debts expense account.

Often statistical evidence shows that in a given business a certain proportion of all debts incurred in a given period will probably prove bad, though it is not known which particular debts will lose their value. In such cases a general provision for bad debts is made each year, as a given percentage of the balance sheet value of all debts; this provision is deducted from the total of debtors in preparing the balance sheet. The accounting entries are the same as for the specific provision described in the preceding paragraph.

When a bad debts provision exists, such debts as prove finally bad, and have not been written off earlier, are eliminated by crediting debtors account and debiting the provision account.

It is important to develop a procedure that will enable problems of this type, where adjustments to the trial balance are necessary, to be tackled surely and swiftly without undue risk of error. The following paragraphs sketch out such a procedure.

Decide which items in the trial balance (TB) are to be adjusted. Open up T accounts for these, inserting in the T accounts the balances from the TB, ticking the latter off as this is done. Make the adjustments, taking care always to match debits and credits, ticking off each adjustment required in the list of original information, as it is made. The final balances on the T accounts, together with the remaining (unticked) TB balances, give the figures for the final accounts. As each figure is entered in the profit and loss account or the balance sheet, tick it in the TB or the relevant T account.

If you prefer you can prepare a new TB from the balances in the old TB and in the T accounts, before preparing the final accounts.

Once you are fairly sure of yourself, it is a waste of time to open up T accounts for any balances not to be amended: these can be picked up directly from the TB when you prepare the final accounts.

As you develop facility, you will probably find that, for simple adjustments, you can amend the TB directly and omit the T accounts.

It is often best to draw up a very rough profit and loss account and balance sheet in the first place and from these prepare the fair copy.

Never allow debits and credits to be out of balance. Whenever you record a debit, record at the same time a corresponding credit, or *vice-versa*.

We shall show here only the ledger accounts that record salaries and the liability for accrued salaries, depreciation expense and depreciation provision, trade debtors, bad debts expense and bad debts provision. The accounts in question are:

Salaries (expense)		*Salaries* *(liability for amounts accrued)*	
	£		£
Balance b/d	1,300	Salaries (expense)	15
Liability for amounts accrued	15		
	1,315		

Depreciation (expense)		*Depreciation provision*	
	£		£
Depreciation provision	156	Balance b/d	496
		Depreciation expense	156
			652

Trade debtors				*Bad debts provision*			
	£		£		£		£
Balance b/d	1,124	Bad debts provision	24	Trade debtors	24	Balance b/d	24
		Balance c/d	1,100	Balance c/d	55	Bad debts expense	55
	1,124		1,124		79		79
Balance b/d	1,100					Balance b/d	55[1]

Bad debts expense		
	£	
Bad debts provision	55	

1 This is 5% of £1,100.

When the next payment of salaries is made, in the following accounting period, the debit that corresponds to the cash credit entered, can, so far as it relates to the liability for accrued salaries at the end of the previous accounting period, be made to the account for this liability shown above; alternatively, the balance on the latter can, for convenience, be re-transferred to the salaries account in the new period, so that all debits can in the new period be made to the salaries account. In practice, however, the two accounts may be merged, so that at the year-end the salaries account serves as a creditors account as well as an expense account.[1] The final reports are as follows:

AB

Trading and profit and loss account
Year to 31 December 19—

		£	£
	Sales *less* returns		10,870
less	Cost of sales		7,063
			3,807
less	Salaries	1,315	
	General expenses	948	
	Depreciation	156	
	Bad debts provision	55	
			2,474
	Net profit		1,333

Balance sheet, 31 December 19—

		£	£
	Furniture and equipment		
	Cost	1,560	
less	Depreciation	652	
			908
	Current assets		
	Stock	1,700	
	Trade debtors	1,045[2]	
	Cash at bank and in hand	387	
			3,132
			4,040

1 The ledger accounts for adjustments of this kind are discussed further in the last section of this chapter.
2 £1,100−£55=£1,045.

	£	£
less Current liabilities		
Trade creditors	782	
Accrued expenses	15	
	—	797
Net assets		3,243
Capital		
Balance, 1 January 19—		2,420
Profit for year		1,333
		3,753
less Drawings		510
Balance, 31 December 19—		3,243

Example 5

From the following trial balance of the *XY* Club, and the other information provided, prepare the club's final accounts (income and expenditure account[1] and balance sheet) for the year to 31 December 19—:

	£	£
Surplus, 1 January[2]		750
Investments at cost	560	
Cash at bank	56	
Petty cash[3]	16	
Stock of unsold journals, 1 January	130	
Interest on investments		28
Subscriptions		470
Salary of secretary	400	
Stationery, postage, etc.	31	
Rent	60	
Printing expenses of journal for year 19—	85	
Sale of journals		90
	1,338	1,338

1 *Income and expenditure account* is often used instead of *profit and loss account* for non-profit-making enterprises.

2 This is equivalent to the capital account of the sole trader. It measures the surplus of assets over liabilities – the accumulated 'wealth' of the club to date.

3 This is the term used for relatively small amounts of coin and notes held in order to facilitate payment of minor or 'petty' expenses for which it is not convenient to draw cheques.

The following matters have not yet been recorded in the accounts and are therefore not reflected in the trial balance figures:

(*a*) The market value of investments at 31 December was £520. The ledger value is not to be altered, but the market value is to be noted on the balance sheet. (This is the normal practice.)

(*b*) Of the stock of journals, including those printed during the year, copies valued in the books (i.e. in the ledger) at £90 were sold during the year. (Show the net profit or loss from the journal for the year as a single item in the account, with revenue and expense inset.)

(*c*) At 31 December, rent of £20 was owing for the last quarter of the year.

(*d*) At 31 December, subscriptions for the year still unpaid amounted to £30.

Here we have to apply our principles to a new form of organization. This should cause no serious trouble if we know the principles thoroughly. Calculate the effect of the adjustments necessitated by (*b*), (*c*) and (*d*) by using T accounts (ticking off the opening balances for these in the trial balance and obtaining new balances on these accounts) and prepare a new rough trial balance *after* the adjustments to prove your arithmetic. The printing expenses should be transferred to the stock account as an increase in the balance sheet value of the journals. The adjustment for cost of sales can then be made. Then prepare the income and expenditure account exactly as you would a profit and loss account. (There is no trading section in the usual sense, though the section showing the financial results of the publishing of the journal is a kind of trading account.) Add the net surplus ('profit') or deficit ('loss') for the year to the opening surplus in the balance sheet to arrive at the final surplus or deficit.

The ledger account form of report presentation has been used here for illustrative purposes. In practice, however, it would usually be better to use the more easily understood narrative form of previous examples.

The solution is as follows:

Adjustments:

(b)   *Stock of journals*

	£		£
Balance b/d	130	Transfer to	
Expenses	85	cost of	
		sales	90
		Balance c/d	125
	215		215
Balance b/d	125		

Journal expenses

	£		£
Balance b/d	85	Transfer to	
		stock	85

Journals: cost of sales

	£
Transfer from	
stock	90

(c)   *Rent (expense)*

	£
Balance b/d	60
Liability	20
	80

Rent (liability)

		£
	Expense	20

(d)   *Subscriptions (revenue)*

		£
	Balance b/d	470
	Debtors	30
		500

Subscriptions (debtors)

	£	
Subscription		
revenue	30	

Final accounts:

XY Club
Income and expenditure account
Year to 31 December 19—

	£		£	£
Salary of secretary	400	Subscriptions		500
Rent	80	Investment income		28
Stationery, postage, etc.	31	Sale of journals	90	
Surplus for year	17[1]	*less* Cost of sales	90	
	528			528

1 This is the balance. In reports of this kind (as distinct from the ledger accounts themselves) it is not usual to show the 'brought-down' part of the profit balance below the line.

Balance sheet, 31 December 19—

	£		£
Rent due	20	Petty cash	16
Surplus		Cash at bank	56
Balance 1 January	750	Investments at cost (market	
Surplus for year	17	value at 31 December	
	767	19— £520)	560
		Debtors for subscriptions	30
		Stock of journals[1]	125
	787		787

Example 6

The following estimated data relate to a manufacturing business which is to begin operations on 1 January 19—. You are required to show how much money must be paid in by the owners as capital in order to finance the business until the following 31 March. Show also the profit and loss calculation. Prove your work by constructing the balance sheet at 31 March 19—.

Data

	£
Fixed assets to be bought and paid for in January	
Freehold factory	4,000
Machinery and equipment	10,000
Furniture, fittings, etc.	2,500
Motor vehicles	3,000
Raw materials bought	
February (to be paid for in March)	1,000
March (to be paid for in April)	2,000
Wages of operatives engaged on production, to be treated as part of the value of work in progress	
February	800
March	1,200
Salaries, non-manufacturing wages, and other expenses not to be treated as part of the value of work in progress, i.e. not to be regarded as creating balance sheet value	
January	200
February	300
March	300

1 It would be good practice to explain how these had been valued.

£

Balance sheet value (cost) of raw material used for production	
February	400
March	600
Balance sheet value (cost) of finished goods produced	
March	2,300
Balance sheet value (cost) of finished goods sold	
March	1,800
Sales value of finished goods sold	
March (to be paid for in April)	2,800
Cash balance at bank at 31 March is required to be at least	1,500

Depreciation on the fixed assets (factory, machinery, equipment, furniture, fittings, and motor vehicles) can be ignored.

Here we have a new type of problem. We are asked, now, not to prepare a set of accounts for events that have taken place but to forecast how the accounts will appear *if* certain events happen: that is, to construct a *budget*. However, the principles that have been used for the first kind of problem can be applied equally well to the second.

The problem is to ascertain the amount of cash to be paid in that will just leave a balance of £1,500 on 31 March. This can be found by first constructing a hypothetical cash account for the period on the assumption that the opening balance is zero and that any excess of payments over receipts can be treated as a bank overdraft. The cash to be paid in will be equal to the highest level of credit balance (i.e. overdraft) shown on this hypothetical cash account during the period, *plus* the amount, if any, needed to bring the closing balance shown up to £1,500 debit. We can ignore depreciation as this does not involve a cash outlay.

We solve the problem here by constructing T accounts for the three months. (In practice, of course, this would be done on working papers and not, as with ordinary accounts, in the formal business records.)

The solution is as follows:

Cash at bank

		£
Jan	Factory	4,000
,,	Machinery, etc.	10,000
,,	Furniture, etc.	2,500
,,	Motor vehicles	3,000
,,	Salaries, etc.	200
Feb	,, ,,	300
,,	Work in progress	800
Mar	,, ,, ,,	1,200
,,	Salaries, etc.	300
,,	Creditors	1,000
		23,300

Freehold factory

	£	
Jan Bank	4,000	

Machinery and equipment

	£	
Jan Bank	10,000	

Furniture, fittings, etc.

	£	
Jan Bank	2,500	

Motor vehicles

	£	
Jan Bank	3,000	

Raw materials

		£			£
Feb	Creditors	1,000	Feb	Work in progress	400
Mar	,,	2,000	Mar	,,	600
				Balance c/d	2,000
		3,000			3,000
Balance b/d		2,000			

Salaries and non-manufacturing wages

		£	
Jan Bank		200	
Feb	,,	300	
Mar	,,	300	
		800	

Work in progress

		£			£
Feb	Bank	800	Mar	Finished goods	2,300
,,	Raw materials	400		Balance c/d	700
Mar	,,	600			
,,	Bank	1,200			
		3,000			3,000
Balance b/d		700			

Finished goods

	£		£
Mar Work in pro-gress	2,300	Mar Cost of sales	1,800
		Balance c/d	500
	2,300		2,300
Balance b/d	500		

Cost of sales

	£		
Mar Finished goods	1,800		

Sales

			£
		Mar Debtors	2,800

Creditors

	£		£
Mar Cash	1,000	Feb Raw materials	1,000
Balance c/d	2,000	Mar ,,	2,000
	3,000		3,000
		Balance b/d	2,000

Debtors

	£	
Mar Sales	2,800	

The cash at bank account shows by 31 March a credit balance (i.e. overdraft) of £23,300. That this is the maximum overdraft needed in the three months can be seen by inspection, as there have been no receipts.[1] As the required condition is a *debit* balance of at least £1,500, an additional debit of £23,300 + £1,500 = £24,800 is needed. This gives the answer. We can now debit cash at bank with £24,800 as at 1 January and credit capital with the same amount to give our final budgeted cash account. The final balances on these accounts are then:

[1] Had there been it would have been necessary to calculate the balance month by month (in practice perhaps even day by day).

Cash at bank			Capital		
	£				£
Balance				Balance	
b/d	1,500			b/d	24,800

A trial balance will now show:

	£	£
Cash at bank	1,500	
Capital		24,800
Factory	4,000	
Machinery, etc.	10,000	
Furniture, etc.	2,500	
Motor vehicles	3,000	
Raw materials	2,000	
Salaries, etc.	800	
Work in progress	700	
Finished goods	500	
Cost of sales	1,800	
Sales		2,800
Creditors		2,000
Debtors	2,800	
	29,600	29,600

The profit and loss budget will be:

	£
Sales	2,800
less Cost of sales	1,800
Gross profit	1,000
less General expenses	800
Net profit, subject to depreciation	200

The budgeted balance sheet will be:

	£		£
Capital to be paid in 1 January	24,800	Freehold factory at cost	4,000
Profit (before depreciation) for the three months to 31 March	200	Machinery and equipment at cost	10,000
		Furniture and fittings, etc. at cost	2,500
	25,000	Motor vehicles at cost	3,000
Creditors	2,000		19,500

		£	
	Stocks:		
	Raw materials	2,000	
	Work in progress	700	
	Finished goods	500	
		3,200	
	Debtors	2,800	
	Cash at bank	1,500	
			7,500
	27,000		27,000

Example 7

The accounting reports of clubs and similar bodies often take the form of a single receipts and payments account, that is, a statement in the form of a cash account that summarizes the cash receipts and payments under various heads. This may be quite informative and adequate for the purpose. Nevertheless, if there are other assets than cash, and also liabilities, these may have changed sufficiently in value to alter the financial position significantly: a receipts and payments account will not show this. An income and expenditure account, with a balance sheet, provides a fuller picture. An alternative to preparing these is to provide a list of assets and liabilities as an appendix to the receipts and payments account: this provides more information than the receipts and payments account, but does not show the net change in the value of assets *less* liabilities; and may become unwieldy if the organization's affairs are at all complicated. The following example shows how a receipts and payments account can be converted into a full set of final accounts on double entry principles.

The secretary of the *ZZ* Club has drafted the following receipts and payments account:

Year ended 31 December 19—

Receipts	£	Payments	£
Balance at bank,		Salaries and wages	876
1 January	522	Purchases of liquor	1,366
Subscriptions	896	Rent and rates	86
Sales of liquor	1,783	Light and heat	69
		Balance at bank,	
		31 December	804
	3,201		3,201

The following information is available:

(1) Stock of liquor was valued at £233 at the beginning of the year and at £198 at the end.
(2) The club owed £76 for purchases of liquor on 1 January and £87 at the end of the year.
(3) The club owns equipment. This was valued at £186 on 1 January; the year's depreciation is set at £37.
(4) The payments for light and heat include £7 for electricity for the last quarter of the previous year. The electricity bill for the final quarter of the year of the account has not been paid: it amounts to £12.

Prepare an income and expenditure account for the year and the final balance sheet. Show the net trading results from liquor sales.

The first step in a problem of this kind is to establish the opening debit and credit position. This can be done by preparing an opening trial balance as at 1 January by listing assets and liabilities at that date and finding the opening surplus.

From the opening trial balance and the other data T accounts can be prepared for the period, on working papers. Then balances can be carried down and the final accounts prepared.

Note that here no T account need be prepared for cash: this is already provided in the question; all that is necessary is to complete the double entry by 'posting' each cash receipt or payment to the appropriate account.

Be careful to tick off items as a check on the completeness of the double entry: as the T accounts are opened tick off the balances entered in these against the items in the opening trial balance; tick off the cash balance in the opening TB against the opening balance in the receipts and payments summary; as the debit and credit aspect of the cash credits and debits are completed, tick the latter off in the receipts and payments summary; as the balance sheet is prepared tick off the items in the final TB.

The opening trial balance is as follows:

	£	£
Cash	522	
Stock	233	
Trade creditors		76
Heat and light (accrued expense)		7
Equipment	186	
	941	83
Surplus (by difference)		858
	941	941

Double entry T accounts (except for cash, which is already given in the question) are as follows:

Stock

	£		£
Balance b/d	233	Cost of sales	1,412[1]
Creditors	1,377	Balance c/d	198
	1,610		1,610
Balance b/d	198		

Trade creditors

	£		£
Cash	1,366	Balance b/d	76
Balance c/d	87	Stock	1,377[1]
	1,453		1,453
		Balance b/d	87

Equipment

	£		£
Balance b/d	186	I & E (Depn.)	37
		Balance c/d	149
	186		186
Balance b/d	149		

Light and heat

	£		£
Cash	69	Balance b/d	7
Balance c/d	12	I & E	74[1]
	81		81
		Balance b/d	12

1 These figures are obtained by inserting the amount needed to make the two sides of the account balance (see below).

Surplus

£		£
	Balance b/d	858
	I & E	194
		1,052

Income and expenditure

	£		£
Salaries, etc.	876	Subscriptions	896
Rent, etc.	86	Sales	1,783
Light, etc.	74		
Depreciation	37		
Cost of sales	1,412		
Surplus	194		
	2,679		2,679

Closing trial balance:

	£	£
Cash	804	
Stock	198	
Trade creditors		87
Heat and light (accrued expense)		12
Equipment	149	
Surplus		1,052
	1,151	1,151

Purchases of stock are derived by difference on the trade creditors account, the opening and closing balances, and the cash paid for purchases, being known; once purchases have been calculated the corresponding entry in the stock account can be made. The cost of sales and the light and heat expense are similarly derived by difference.

In the above working solution the closing trial balance summarizes the balance sheet position after balancing the income and expenditure account. It is, of course, possible to prepare a trial balance before the income account is drafted; but here it hardly seems worthwhile.

It is also hardly worthwhile here opening separate T accounts for salaries, rent, and depreciation. These can be entered directly into the income and expenditure account.

The final accounts as they might be presented to the club members are as follows:

ZZ Club
Income and expenditure account
Year ended 31 December 19—

	£		£	£
Salaries and wages	876	Subscriptions		896
Rent and rates	86	Net profit on liquor		
Light and heat	74	sales:		
Depreciation	37	Sales	1,783	
Surplus for year	194	*less* Cost of sales	1,412	
				371
	1,267			1,267

Balance sheet
as at 31 December 19—

	£		£	£
Surplus		Equipment		149
Balance 1 January 19—	858			
Surplus for 19—	194	Stock of liquor	198	
		Cash at bank	804	
Balance 31 Dec 19—	1,052			1,002
	£			
Trade creditors	87			
Accrued expense	12			
	99			
	1,151			1,151

Example 8

Our next example is designed to give a further indication of the way in which accounting reports may be used. It calls for the preparation of an accounting report and for a discussion of the economic significance of the figures in the report.

A business has the following balance sheet at the beginning of a given year:

	£		£	£
Capital	1,600	Equipment at cost	1,600	
Creditors	400	*less* Depreciation	600	
				1,000
		Stock	500	
		Debtors	300	
		Cash	200	
				1,000
	2,000			2,000

The following forecasts are made of the trading results for the year:

	£
Sales	2,800
Purchases	2,000
Stock (valued at cost) at end of year	400
General expenses (all paid in cash)	1,100
Depreciation of equipment	200

The debtors for sales at the end of the year (included in the above sales figure) are estimated at £350.

The creditors for stock supplied (included in the above purchases figure) are estimated at £400.

The owner is not sure of the financial implications of these figures. He asks you, as accountant, whether you have any advice to offer him. He also tells you he does not intend to make any drawings during the year.

Advise the owner:

(1) On the expected financial position, i.e. the position with respect to cash needs.
(2) What special action, if any, this position calls for.

Analyse the year's expected transactions, using schematic double entry T accounts, and prepare a final balance sheet.

Cost of sales can be found by difference as the closing stock is known. The cash received from debtors and paid to creditors can be deduced in the same way, since the closing debtors and creditors are known.

Here again the T accounts would be working figures and would not be part of a formal set of records.

The solution is as follows. We have eliminated separate revenue and expense accounts from the working figures as redundant in this example: sales revenue, and expenses, are entered directly in the profit and loss account.

<table>
<tr><td colspan="3" align="center">Cash</td><td colspan="3" align="center">Debtors</td></tr>
<tr><td></td><td>£</td><td>£</td><td></td><td>£</td><td>£</td></tr>
<tr><td>Balance
b/d</td><td>200</td><td>General
expenses 1,100</td><td>Balance
b/d</td><td>300</td><td>Cash 2,750
Balance</td></tr>
<tr><td>Debtors</td><td>2,750</td><td>Creditors 2,000</td><td>Profit and
loss</td><td></td><td>b/d 350</td></tr>
<tr><td>Balance
c/d</td><td>150</td><td></td><td>(sales)</td><td>2,800</td><td></td></tr>
<tr><td></td><td>3,100</td><td>3,100</td><td></td><td>3,100</td><td>3,100</td></tr>
<tr><td></td><td></td><td>Balance
b/d 150</td><td>Balance
b/d</td><td>350</td><td></td></tr>
</table>

<table>
<tr><td colspan="3" align="center">Creditors</td><td colspan="3" align="center">Stock</td></tr>
<tr><td></td><td>£</td><td>£</td><td></td><td>£</td><td>£</td></tr>
<tr><td>Cash</td><td>2,000</td><td>Balance</td><td>Balance b/d 500</td><td></td><td>Profit and</td></tr>
<tr><td>Balance
c/d</td><td>400</td><td>b/d 400
Stock 2,000</td><td>Creditors 2,000</td><td></td><td>loss
(cost of
sales) 2,100</td></tr>
<tr><td></td><td>2,400</td><td>2,400</td><td></td><td></td><td>Balance
c/d 400</td></tr>
<tr><td></td><td></td><td>Balance
b/d 400</td><td></td><td>2,500</td><td>2,500</td></tr>
<tr><td></td><td></td><td></td><td>Balance
b/d</td><td>400</td><td></td></tr>
</table>

<table>
<tr><td colspan="3" align="center">Capital</td><td colspan="3" align="center">Equipment</td></tr>
<tr><td></td><td></td><td>£</td><td></td><td>£</td><td>£</td></tr>
<tr><td></td><td></td><td>Balance
b/d 1,600</td><td>Balance
b/d</td><td>1,000</td><td>Profit and
loss
(depre-
ciation) 200</td></tr>
<tr><td></td><td></td><td></td><td></td><td></td><td>Balance
c/d 800</td></tr>
<tr><td></td><td></td><td></td><td></td><td>1,000</td><td>1,000</td></tr>
<tr><td></td><td></td><td></td><td>Balance
b/d</td><td>800</td><td></td></tr>
</table>

<table>
<tr><td colspan="4" align="center">Profit and loss account</td></tr>
<tr><td></td><td>£</td><td></td><td>£</td></tr>
<tr><td>Stock (cost of sales)</td><td>2,100</td><td>Debtors (sales)</td><td>2,800</td></tr>
<tr><td>Cash (general expenses)</td><td>1,100</td><td>Balance (loss) c/d</td><td>600</td></tr>
<tr><td>Equipment (depreciation)</td><td>200</td><td></td><td></td></tr>
<tr><td></td><td>3,400</td><td></td><td>3,400</td></tr>
<tr><td>Balance b/d</td><td>600</td><td></td><td></td></tr>
</table>

Estimated balance sheet at 31 December 19—

	£	£		£	£
Capital 1 January		1,600	Equipment at		
less Loss for year		600	cost	1,600	
		——	less Depreciation	800	
		1,000		——	800
Creditors	400		Stock	400	
Bank overdraft (or			Debtors	350	
other source of				——	750
finance)	150				
	——	550			
		1,550			1,550

Estimated trading and profit and loss report
Year to 31 December 19—

	£	£
Sales		2,800
less Cost of sales		2,100
		——
Gross profit		700
less General expenses	1,100	
Depreciation	200	
	——	1,300
Loss for year		600

There are two main points to be brought out:

(1) Profit and loss. Unless gross profit can be increased considerably or expenses cut heavily it will be unprofitable to trade. Moreover, the economic loss may be greater than the accounts show if, as is presumably the case, the accounting expenses include nothing in respect of the owner's return on his invested capital or his services.

Suppose that the return required on the investment (that is, the return which, after allowing for differing risks, measures the best rate that could be earned by using the resources in other ways) is considered to be 10% per annum, and that the balance sheet valuations are fairly good approximations to market value. Then the annual return required is about £160. Suppose also that the expenses include a manager's salary and that the owner assesses his own remuneration for the general control of business policy (the 'entrepreneurial services') at £300 per annum. (We can assume that the business, being a small one, only consumes a small part of his time.) Then we can say that until the accounting profit reaches a level of £460 per annum £(160 + 300) there is no economic profit (assuming the other accounting figures, especially depreciation, are reasonably good measures of the economic costs).

(2) *Finance.* It will not be possible to keep the business in operation unless additional external finance can be obtained, from the bank or elsewhere, of at least £150. (Presumably rather more may be needed to allow for contingencies; this could be dealt with, for example, by the granting of greater overdraft facilities by the bank.)

On a short term view it is unlikely, however, that the owner will wish to put more money in, since the return before allowing for the cost of any additional finance is already negative. For the same reason it may not be easy to obtain finance from other sources even on loan; the figures suggest that the risk of default on interest and repayment is high.

On the other hand, it is not enough to consider only the short term view. It may be worthwhile keeping the assets together in the expectation of better times later; and if so, it is likely that it will be worthwhile continuing to trade in order to maintain the organization as a whole, including its connections with suppliers and purchasers. (This is called 'maintaining the goodwill'.)

It is likely that some of the accounting expenses, including depreciation, are unavoidable in the short run if the business is not to be closed, and to the extent that this is true they should be disregarded in computing the economic loss or gain from closing temporarily. The same is true of the interest on capital and the owner's remuneration. This might lead us to two kinds of calculation as given at the top of the next page.

These show that (1) it is not worthwhile continuing in the long run unless gross profit (the *contribution* to the overhead costs) is at least £1,760; but (2) this year the cost of keeping open, *provided that the business is to be continued thereafter* (so that the premises, etc. cannot be abandoned), is only £800 (presumably for wages, etc.). As the gross profit is £700, the net sacrifice from keeping

	A Long run costs	B Short run costs (one year)
	£	£
Accounting expenses (other than cost of sales)[1]	1,300	1,300
Additional economic costs:		
Owner's remuneration, say	300	—
Interest on investment, say 10% on £1,600	160	—
	1,760	1,300
less Expenses that could not be saved by closing down for one year (such as rent, insurance, depreciation, etc.), let us say	—	500
Economic (or 'opportunity') cost	1,760	800

open and trading this year is only £100. This may be worthwhile incurring if it improves future prospects.

This brings out the very important point that economic costs must be considered *in relation to particular decisions*.

It must also be remembered that, in business, estimates usually have to be very approximate: we must not be fooled by the accuracy of the arithmetic. In the last resort personal judgement must also be applied. The figures help, but are not decisive.

Adjustments for final accounts

We shall conclude this chapter by considering at greater length certain practical points that arise when final accounts are prepared. When a profit and loss account and balance sheet are drafted, whether at the end of a financial year or some shorter period, it is necessary, as we have seen, to enter liabilities for expenses that are accruing (such as rent and electricity) but have not yet been recorded, because payment is not yet legally due; and similar adjustments are made where amounts already

1 We assume that all these are economic costs that could be saved in the longer run if the business closed.

paid have purchased benefits extending beyond the end of the period of account.

In such instances when, in the ensuing period, the full liability is known, e.g. when the bill is received, it will include the part accrued at the end of the earlier financial period; the liability (and expense) to be recorded at this later date, are, therefore, smaller by the amount previously accrued. Thus, suppose that in a given business the electricity expense accrued at 31 December 1962, the balance sheet date, is £30, and that the electricity bill received later, for the three months ended on 31 January 1963, is £50. It follows that the expense to be recorded in the accounts for the March quarter is £20 (plus, of course, any amount accrued from 1 February to 31 March); and this £20, added to the liability of £30 at 31 December, raises the liability at 31 January to the amount of the bill, £50.

Again, at the end of a period one of the assets may be a payment in advance, representing the accrued value of benefits already paid for but not yet enjoyed; when the benefits are enjoyed in the next period this asset must be reduced and a corresponding expense recorded. Suppose that the amount of rent paid in advance at 31 December, representing the benefits of occupation from 1 January to 28 February, is £40. It follows that in the accounts for the March quarter the rent expense must include this £40, and during this period the asset value recorded at 31 December, under the head of payments in advance, will disappear.

If we use special liability and asset accounts in the formal book-keeping system to record, respectively, the amounts accrued and paid in advance at the balance sheet date, we usually reverse the book-keeping entries in order to eliminate the amounts in question from those accounts immediately after that date, in such a way that the amount accrued or paid in advance is left as a credit or debit in the *expense* account in the new period[1]; this is demonstrated in the following examples, in which the figures are the same as those used above. We shall assume the bill for electricity to 31 January is paid on 14 February. We show only the expense accounts and the asset or liability accounts for payments in advance or accruals.

1 The object is to simplify the formal book-keeping or data processing routine, discussed in Chapter 8.

Accrual:

Electricity expense

1962		£	1962		£
31 Dec	Balance b/d	x	31 Dec	Profit and loss $(30+x)$	
	Electricity Board	30			
1963			1963		
31 Jan	Electricity Board	50	1 Jan	Electricity Board	30

Electricity Board

1963		£	1962		£
1 Jan	Electricity expense	30	31 Dec	Electricity expense	30
			1963		
14 Feb	Cash	50	31 Jan	Electricity expense	50

Payment in advance:

Rent expense

1962		£	1962		£
31 Dec	Balance b/d	y	31 Dec	Rent in advance	40
				Profit and loss $(y-40)$	
1963					
1 Jan	Rent in advance	40			

Rent in advance

1962		£	1963		£
31 Dec	Rent expense	40	1 Jan	Rent expense	40

It is often considered simpler, however, to make all end of period adjustments of the above type in the expense accounts themselves; the ledger accounts for the above examples would then appear as follows:

Accrual:

Electricity expense

1962		£	1962		£
31 Dec	Balance b/d	x	31 Dec	Profit and loss $(30+x)$	
	Balance c/d	30			
1963					
31 Jan	Electricity board	50	31 Dec	Balance b/d	30

Electricity Board

1963		£	1963		£
14 Feb	Cash	50	31 Jan	Electricity Board	

Payment in advance:

Rent expense

1962		£	1962		£
31 Dec	Balance b/d	y	31 Dec	Profit and loss	$(y-40)$
				Balance c/d	40
31 Dec	Balance b/d	40			

Here the electricity expense account is also acting as a creditor account at balance sheet date, and the rent expense account is also acting as an asset account at that date.

The same kind of problem arises in connection with revenue received in advance. If a revenue such as rent receivable from the letting of property is received in advance of the services yielded in exchange for it, it is conventional to regard the amount 'unearned' (obtained by making a time apportionment) as measuring the liability to provide those services in the following period; the cash has been received, but there is still a liability to provide services. One could put the point in another way by saying that since these services will absorb resources later they may be regarded as reducing, *pro tanto*, the value of the business at the balance sheet date, so that their anticipated cost should be recorded as a claim or negative asset. Assume that a shop owned by the business is let and that, before 31 December 1962, rent of £900 is received in respect of the three months to 31 January 1963. If final accounts are prepared at 31 December, a liability of £300 would be recorded at that date, and the revenue to be credited to profit and loss account would be reduced to £600.

The account would be:

Rent receivable

1962		£	1962		£
31 Dec	Profit and loss	600	31 Dec	Balance b/d	900
	Balance c/d	300			
			31 Dec	Balance b/d	300

Accruals of revenue can also arise. Their treatment is analagous to that of accruals of expenses.

PART II

DATA FLOW. INTERPRETATION

CONTROL ACCOUNTS.
SUBORDINATE LEDGERS.
ORIGINAL RECORDS.[1]

General

Textbooks on book-keeping and accounts have traditionally devoted a good deal of space to what are called the *books of original entry*: the books or other records in which the raw data are assembled and classified before they are entered in the formal double entry system of ledger accounts. On the other hand our primary interest in this book is in the general principles of double entry book-keeping, and in the balance sheet and profit and loss account, rather than in the original records and sources of information. However, a general appreciation of the process of data collection and classification which links the raw data to the formal accounting system seems likely to be useful, even for those readers who are not concerned with technical accounting details. Those who wish to proceed later to the study of book-keeping and data processing systems in greater detail should understand the nature of the link between the formal accounting system and the sources of accounting data.

We shall indicate here the overall pattern of modern accounting systems. Our discussion will be general and will be appropriate to both modern electronic systems and traditional handwritten ones. In particular, it will introduce the concept of control accounts, fundamental in any modern accounting system, but relatively neglected in most introductory texts.

1 This chapter may be omitted by those not interested in the detail of the book-keeping process without impairing their chances of understanding the last chapter.

Control accounts

The formal double entry system that we have studied in the earlier chapters is the basis of virtually all modern accounting systems. Many of the ledger accounts making up the system must be regarded as what are called *total* or *control* accounts. That is, they summarize a set of transactions that are also recorded in greater detail in what may be called *subordinate* or *detailed* ledger accounts, that is, in ledger accounts that have the same form as the control accounts, but are not part of the formal double entry system.[1] Let us take a simple example. In a particular business the double entry ledger control account for trade creditors, for one day, appears as follows:

Trade creditors

	£		£
Cash	400	Balance b/d	2,000
Balance c/d	1,900	Stock	300
	2,300		2,300
		Balance b/d	1,900

On examining the detailed subordinate accounts of the trade creditors ledger we find three accounts, each in the name of a separate person, which for the same day appear as follows:

J. Brown

		£
Balance b/d		1,600
Stock		200
		1,800

J. Doe

	£
Stock	100

R. Roe

	£		£
Cash	400	Balance b/d	400

1 Some accountants may prefer an alternative interpretation, whereby the detailed accounts are part of the formal double entry system and the control accounts are memorandum records. This does not affect the accounting procedures, but is less elegant as a theoretical basis than the interpretation we adopt here.

The opening balances of the three subordinate accounts sum as follows:

	£
Brown	1,600
Doe	—
Roe	400
	2,000

This total agrees with the opening balance of the control account.

The purchases of stock from these suppliers sum as follows:

	£
Brown	200
Doe	100
Roe	—
	300

This total agrees with the figure shown for stock purchases on the credit side of the control account.

The cash paid to the creditors is as follows:

	£
Brown	—
Doe	—
Roe	400
	400

This total agrees with the control account debit for cash.

Finally the closing balances of the subordinate ledger, when extracted, agree in sign and magnitude with the balance of the control account:

Credit balances	
	£
Brown	1,800
Doe	100
Roe	—
	1,900

These three accounts stand for what in practice may be a very large number of individual accounts, all relating to one class of liability, the entries in which are summarized by the entry of totals in the control account.

This relationship between the control accounts (which provide directly the data for reports for management, shareholders, and others) and the detailed subordinate ledger accounts[1] is typical of modern accounting systems. The detailed accounts provide the legal and arithmetical proof for the total or control accounts, and form the basis for the day-to-day control over such matters as payments to creditors, collection of money from debtors, security of cash and raw materials, and so on. The control accounts accumulate the main accounting magnitudes which have relevance for overall economic control and for certain legal purposes (such as tax assessment). By virtue of the way in which their compilation is organized, the two types of account provide a mutual check on one another's accuracy.[2]

We can, therefore, when we use balance sheets and profit and loss accounts, reflect that the numerical aggregates that appear under the various headings are supported by a host of detailed records which follow in principle the same general form as those we have described in earlier chapters.

In order to demonstrate more fully the way in which the contents of the ledger control accounts, and of the detailed accounts they summarize, are related, and how both are derived from the records that form the statistical raw material of the accounting process, we shall now consider at greater length the process of building up the creditors control account, the detailed accounts of the creditors ledger (each class of items in which, when summed, gives an item in the control account), the stock control account, and the detailed accounts of the stock ledger.

This description will be as general as possible: it will show the features likely to be common to most good systems whether manual, machine, or electronic. It will not describe a particular system. If the principles are understood, students will find they

1 It should be emphasized that though these will have a one-to-one correspondence in pattern with the control account, their actual physical form may vary widely, from written traditional ledger pages to impressions on magnetic tape.

2 This is part of what is called *internal check*.

have little difficulty in applying them to other sections of the business, and to particular situations.

The design of the data flow system

Let us suppose that we have to design an appropriate system and are now considering some typical transactions with this in mind. The primary evidence of a purchase will usually be the supplier's invoice (bill) for the goods in question. Our first step must be to arrange a procedure whereby invoices, as they are received, are checked for accuracy with respect to the following points:[1]

(1) The actual delivery of the goods, in good condition and in conformity with the specification in the original order to the supplier.
(2) The price.
(3) The arithmetical accuracy of any calculations and additions.

The invoice must also be checked off against the purchasing department's record of goods ordered, to show that the order has now been satisfied.

The total of the invoice can now be entered in the accounting system. Let us suppose that 100 such invoices, all checked and passed for entry in the books, have been accumulated and that the total value of the invoices has been obtained, e.g. on an adding machine. We have to ask ourselves how much of the information on the invoice needs to be recorded and in what manner. The principles we have studied in the earlier chapters tell us that the effect of the transaction on the balance sheet, and therefore in the double entry system, must be (a) to increase stock and (b) to increase trade creditors. If an invoice is for £100, the ledger entries, described in T account form, are:

Stock		Trade creditors	
£	£	£	£
Creditors 100	—	—	Stock 100

or, if described in journal form:

	£	£
Stock	100	
Trade creditors		100

1 In a good system each unit of clerical or accounting work is assigned to a particular person, so that responsibilities are always clear.

The date of the transaction may be important. We may wish to know whether it falls before, or after, a given date which happens to be the end of an accounting period. We may also wish to maintain a record of the dates of transactions with particular suppliers, e.g. because this affects the date when payment is due. Hence we must record the date assigned to the entry explicitly[1] or else make sure that each transaction can be indirectly identified with a date, e.g. by allotting to each entry a distinctive code number, or by classifying entries in sets all of which can be seen to fall within given time limits. (This could be done by entering all the February items of an account in a section of the account identified with February.)

We shall also want to identify particular entries with (a) the supplier's name and (b) the type or types of goods. (An invoice for one total amount, identified with one supplier, may relate to several different types of stock.)

We can achieve these aims by:

(1) Entering the total value of all our invoices on the credit side of the control account for *trade creditors*, with the date noted.
(2) Entering the total value of all our invoices on the debit side of the control account for *stock*, with the date noted.
(3) Entering the total value of the invoices relating to a given supplier, say X, on the credit side of the subordinate creditors account for X, with the date noted, and similarly for all other suppliers in the batch.
(4) Entering the total value of the invoices relating to the stock of a given good, say M, on the debit side of the subordinate stock account for M, with the date noted, and similarly for all other types of stock in the batch.
(5) Providing procedural checks as part of the routine of work to ensure that the total value of all items entered under each of (1), (2), (3), and (4) is the same as the original total value of the invoices.

Traditionally, this procedure was carried out by the use of special journals or *day books*, which provided for the analysis and arithmetical check needed; now it is more likely to form part of a system of mechanical or electronic accounting.

The traditional term 'entry' has been used as a shorthand

1 This need not be the actual day the entry is made.

expression for 'making a specified record'. This record need not be written. In the case of (3) above, for example, it may be convenient to use the invoices themselves, suitably sorted and filed, for the record of the amounts owing to each individual supplier. Or the records for (3) and (4) could take the form of punched cards derived from the original invoices, while (1) and (2) were typewritten cards or sheets, obtained by tabulating the punched cards.

The detailed records of (3), combined with all other such records, would constitute the creditors ledger (sometimes called the *purchases* or *bought* ledger). The total in this ledger, for each type of entry in a given period, must sum to the amount of the same type of entry in the creditors control account in the same period.

Similarly the detailed records of (4) support the totals in the stock control account.

These procedures are illustrated in diagrammatic form in Diagram 1. In this diagram the control accounts, forming part of the formal double entry system from which the balance sheet is built up, are enclosed in square boxes. Subordinate ledger accounts are not so enclosed.

The general outlines of data flow systems for other types of transaction are sketched out in Diagrams 2 to 5. These are drawn up on the same lines as Diagram 1 and should be interpreted accordingly. They relate respectively to records of expenses and expense creditors; of sales and debtors; of cash receipts; and of cash payments. These, together with Diagram 1, cover the main aspects of a simple trading company which maintains systematic stock records.[1] The extension of these principles to special cases should cause little difficulty once the general pattern is understood.

It may be noted that Diagram 2 differs from 1 only in that it relates to expenses and expense creditors. No question of stock arises in this case. The debits are made directly to the main expense accounts. Detailed subordinate accounts are less likely to be needed for expenses and are not shown in the diagram,

1 The usual assumption made in book-keeping and accounting texts, namely that no systematic stock records will be kept, seems most unsatisfactory, in that the model chosen for instruction is that of the worst practice.

DIAGRAM 1

PURCHASES

SOURCE OF INFORMATION: SUPPLIERS' INVOICES

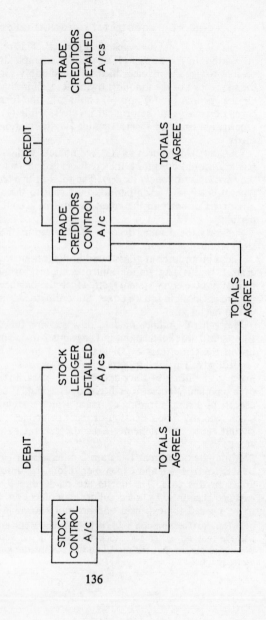

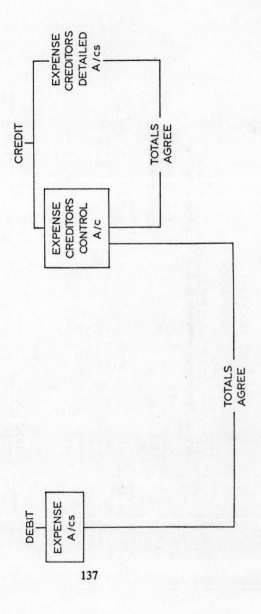

DIAGRAM 2

EXPENSES

SOURCE OF INFORMATION : SUPPLIERS' INVOICES

CREDIT

EXPENSE
CREDITORS
DETAILED
A/cs

EXPENSE
CREDITORS
CONTROL
A/c

TOTALS
AGREE

DEBIT

EXPENSE
A/cs

TOTALS
AGREE

DIAGRAM 3

SALES

SOURCE OF INFORMATION: COPIES OF SALES INVOICES SENT TO CUSTOMERS

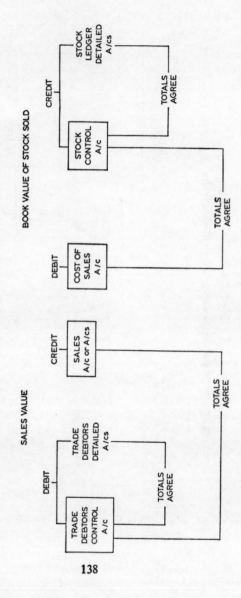

DIAGRAM 4

CASH RECEIPTS

SOURCE OF INFORMATION: CHEQUES, NOTES AND COIN RECEIVED AND BANKED

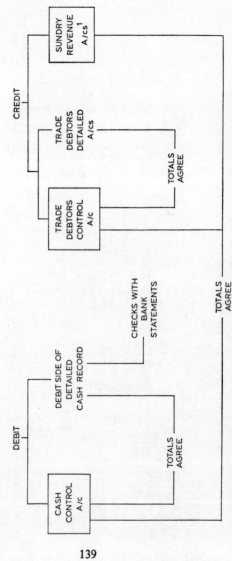

1 These will be credited for such items as interest on investments for which no previous debt is recorded.

DIAGRAM 5

CASH PAYMENTS

SOURCE OF INFORMATION: COUNTERFOILS OF CHEQUES DRAWN FOR PAYMENTS

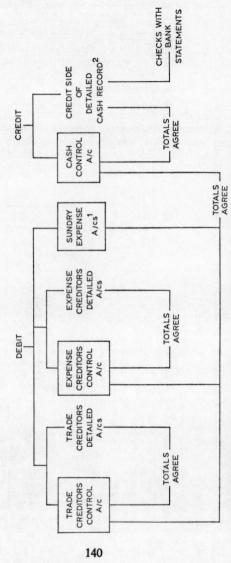

1 These will be debited for expenses in respect of which no previous liability has been set up.
2 Such payments as wages will be shown in total on the day of payment and will be supported by detailed schedules.

though they could be used as a means of reducing the detail in the main ledger accounts. A main double entry ledger account – enclosed in a square in the diagrams – is only described as a 'control account' where there are detailed subordinate accounts supporting it.

Diagram 3 gives the system for sales and debtors. It is in some respects similar to Diagram 1 looked at from the view point of a seller rather than a buyer, but in it the recording, at cost price, of the goods removed from stock is separated from the recording of the sales value. This is necessary in order to obtain separate profit and loss account classifications for sales and for cost of sales.

THE ANALYSIS AND INTERPRETATION
OF ACCOUNTING REPORTS

The purpose of the analysis

The purpose of business accounting reports is to provide numerical information that will help the management, the shareholders or other owners, or other interested parties, to make decisions. The analysis and interpretation of these reports is the critical study of the figures they contain carried out with this purpose in mind. As business (or any other set of economic activities) is a process over time, it follows that the study of change and rates of change in figures is in general more informative than the examination of values at a given moment of time: trends are usually more important than absolute figures.

One of the aims of the analysis is to isolate the causes of changes in revenues and expenses and in the balance sheet structure of assets and liabilities; it is therefore essentially a matter of studying relationships. If, for example, sales revenue rises, the board of directors will wish to know how far this is due to a good sales staff. They therefore compare the change in sales revenue with the change, if any, in the expense of the sales organization. A rise in the ratio of revenue to expense is *prima facie* evidence of higher economic efficiency. The difficulty is that usually other things are changing at the same time. In the above example, changes in general market conditions or in production quality, both of which may affect sales revenue, may confuse the issue. This is why interpretation is difficult and no single test is, in general, significant, taken by itself.[1]

1 Statisticians have techniques that can, in certain instances, be used to separate out the effects of different causes operating at the same time. The use of such methods in business and public administration is not

Any accounting figure can be related to another figure or figures, in:

(1) a previous estimate or budget;
(2) an accounting report for a previous period;
(3) the same accounting report;
(4) an accounting report of some other organization.

Furthermore, any figure can be considered in connection with events inside or external to the enterprise that are not represented by accounting data. The latter point is specially important because no accounting figures can be interpreted with safety unless the general circumstances of the organization at the relevant times are borne in mind.

The results of analysis can be used in two main ways. They can be used in planning future action; and they can be used to determine whether in the past there has been success or failure to maximize the economic opportunities, and on whose part. For the first of these uses the analyst may assume that relationships discovered will hold good in the future, subject to adjustments in respect of known changes in conditions: for example, he may decide that a certain relationship between the level of advertising expenditure and sales will persist. In the second use the analyst is in essence considering, on the basis of earlier experience (as where a ratio between two figures changes over time), or on the basis of his knowledge of the current circumstances, whether relationships discovered indicate a satisfactory state of affairs. He may, for example, after comparing the expenditure on salesmen's salaries and commission for the last three years with the sales revenue for the same period, decide that the results are unsatisfactory, or are becoming less satisfactory. We must never forget, however, the point made above – that there are nearly always many causes operating, and that the apparent cause may not be the true explanation; in the above case the real trouble might be defective products, or a general economic recession.

These two types of application correspond to the two main applications of cost accounting techniques – estimating and budgeting on the one hand, and cost control on the other. We

yet widespread, though we may expect them to be used more in the future. These techniques are, however, still only applicable to a relatively limited number of situations.

are thus led to the conclusion that there is no hard and fast distinction between cost accounting and cost analysis on the one hand and ordinary accounting and the analysis or interpretation of accounts on the other, though we tend to speak about cost analysis when we are concerned with the analysis of particular activities within the enterprise, and of the analysis or interpretation of accounts when we are concerned with the overall results of the enterprise. It is, indeed, characteristic of what is called the analysis and interpretation of accounts that it is often carried out in circumstances when the results will not lead to action within the enterprise, whereas costing studies are normally intended to result in such action. A minority shareholder in a company can interpret the annual accounts that the directors must send him. But if he dislikes what he finds he can do little except sell his shares. Even this distinction, however, is not always valid. A shareholder who held a controlling interest in his company – a shareholding that carried a substantial part of the voting power in shareholders' meetings – could bring effective action to bear on the directors if his interpretation of the company's accounts led him to believe this was desirable.

The form of reports to be analysed

One of the first steps in analysing profit and loss accounts and balance sheets for a number of periods is to arrange them in columnar form (if they have not been drafted in that form), so that each class of figures can be seen as a series over time. The object of the analysis is to interpret the activities of the enterprise; the general aim therefore is to have a separate accounting classification for the results of each significant activity. It is not always easy to decide, however, how this shall be achieved. Alternative classifications are possible; it may be desired, for example, on the one hand to study the total expenditure on advertising particular products in relation to the total sales revenue from those products, and on the other hand to relate the total cost of particular sales departments (each covering a number of products) to their individual sales results. The first type of study requires classification of expenditure by the kind of service purchased – here advertising – and by products; the second by departmental activities inside the enterprise. More than one set of figures must be prepared in such a case. Again, it is not always easy to decide whether a particular type of transaction should be in a separate class by itself. At what point, for example, are sales revenues from exceptional transactions sufficiently abnormal to be shown separately? No final answer can be given on this. It is a problem in some respects like that of designing experiments in scientific work: in the last analysis it depends upon the nature of the enterprise, its special problems, and the task of those who use the figures.

There is often a temptation to provide a relatively fine or detailed analysis in order to avoid the covering up of relevant information; but it is all too easy to reduce reports to an unmanageable mass of detail: one of the main purposes of accounting must not be forgotten – to reduce extensive data to a relatively simple form in order to simplify interpretation. This problem can be dealt with by preparing reports in such a form that the primary statement – say a profit and loss account – is a relatively simple document without a great number of classifications, and by providing supporting schedules in which the primary figures are analysed in substantially greater detail, and possibly in alternative ways.

It is sometimes useful to select a limited number of key figures which can be presented at frequent intervals to those concerned with management, the object being to convey a good general idea of how things are going without including an excess of detail, the study of which will take up valuable time. Such figures will not by themselves tell anyone much about what is happening in the business unless a good deal is known already; but where this is the case they may be very useful. Thus, a director or a manager might well wish to see the full profit and loss account at least once each quarter; but for the intervening months he might be content to receive a simple statement of the sales revenue and the gross and net profit figures, and the percentages of the latter to the sales revenue. If these seemed satisfactory – that is, if they tallied reasonably well with expectations – there would be no need to spend further time on the figures. If they were not satisfactory, more detailed figures could be called for.

Note that for proper interpretation, the accounting classification of assets and liabilities, and revenues and expenses, should remain on the same basis throughout the period of comparison; accountants must always bear this in mind when they are preparing reports and setting up accounting systems to provide the data for these.

Ratios

The elementary statistical device of expressing one figure as a ratio of another has the great advantage of simplifying the study of relationships. Suppose that one finds the sales revenue (the 'turnover') of a business has been as follows over the last four years (in £'s):

11,263   15,372   18,986   23,600

The percentage relations, with the first figure expressed as 100, bring out the trends more clearly than the original figures:

100   136   169   210

One should always be ready to round off figures where this is appropriate; accountants have acquired a bad name for their insistence on a higher degree of apparent accuracy than is needed, and often than is significant. In the above comparison the omission of the last three figures makes the interpretation easier without injuring the analysis. We then have:

11,000   15,000   19,000   24,000

Comparison of actual and budgeted figures

Of the four ways mentioned above in which accounting figures can be related to one another for the purpose of interpretation, the first was the comparison of the figures for a given period with a previous estimate or budget for the same period. This kind of comparison, when carried out systematically, is part of the management technique known as budgetary control. This is an important and interesting subject, but to investigate it at length would take us outside the scope of this book.[1] It will, however, be useful to make a few comments on this topic before we leave it.

The comparison of results with a previous budget will usually show that the organization has done better or worse than was anticipated in the budget. This can of course mean that the budget estimates were wrong; or that the organization has been

1 The subject is discussed at length in my book *Business Budgets and Accounts* (Hutchinson University Library, 1960).

more, or less, efficient than was expected; or that changes have occurred in outside conditions which could not reasonably have been foreseen when the budget was drafted. A variation from the budgeted figure can itself tell us nothing: it can only suggest that further enquiries may be fruitful. Indeed, a close agreement between budget and results may mask unsatisfactory conditions: circumstances may have changed in such a way that results ought to have been better than forecast; or there may have been both bad budgeting and unsatisfactory results, one compensating for the other. The preparation of most budgets requires the co-operation of those who will be responsible later for the actual results and an inefficient subordinate has an interest in setting his target low.

Relationships between reported figures

We turn now to analysis by relating different reported figures of a given business to one another. We shall illustrate this with a simple example, taking the accounting reports of a small company for two successive periods.

The accounts to be analysed are set out in columnar form in Table 9.1 with an additional column for the changes, absolute and relative, from one year to the next. Other relationships examined are shown in Table 9.2.

Sales revenue and gross profit

We start with the profit and loss account. The first figures relate to sales. The sales revenue has increased over the two years by £1,200, or a little less than 12%. On the face of it this is a good sign, suggesting (unless the whole increase is merely due to a rise in the price level)[1] that the company is growing, but it is not a conclusive sign that profit is improving, for costs may have risen more. A person not already aware of the kind of change that might have been expected to occur can do little more at this point than mentally note the change, then passing on to the following items. To anyone, however, who has the original plans of the company in mind, or who has some idea of the growth to be

1 It may well be worthwhile recomputing the sales increase on a constant price level basis by applying an appropriate price index to the figure for one year or the other.

expected, the actual increase will have rather more significance, for it should suggest that the company has done as well as, better, or worse, than was expected. The next step, therefore, would be to look for reasons. Even so, however, a final opinion must be reserved until the remainder of the figures have been examined.

The next item is the cost of sales, defined as in earlier chapters. This, we notice, has risen by £1,000 or rather more than 12%. There is in consequence a rise in gross profit of £200 (£1,200 *less* £1,000). It is not unreasonable to expect that a rise in sales revenue will bring a corresponding rise in the cost of sales; if more goods have been sold, total costs will usually be higher; if the sales revenue has been raised by a rise in selling prices, it is likely that the prices of the goods bought will also have risen.

TABLE 9.1

PROFIT AND LOSS ACCOUNTS

	1961 £	1961 %	1962 £	1962 %	Change £	Change %
Sales	10,200	100·0	11,400	100·0	+ 1,200	+11·8
less Cost of sales[1]	8,200	80·4	9,200	80·7	+ 1,000	+12·2
Gross profit	2,000	19·6	2,200	19·3	+ 200	+10·0
less Administration	730	7·2	790	6·9	+ 60	+ 8·2
Selling and distribution	510	5·0	540	4·7	+ 30	+ 5·9
Finance	310	3·0	400	3·5	+ 90	+29·0
	1,550	15·2	1,730	15·2[2]	+ 180	+11·6
Net profit	450	4·4	470	4·1	+ 20	+ 4·4
add Undistributed profit of previous years	900		1,155		+ 255	
	1,350		1,625		+ 275	
less Dividend for year	195		165		− 30	−15·4
Undistributed profit at end of year	1,155		1,460		+ 305	

	1961	1962
1 We shall assume purchases to be	8,350	9,779
Cost of sales is	8,200	9,200
Therefore stock rise is	150	579

2 The total does not equal the sum of the individual items because these have been rounded off.

BALANCE SHEETS

	31.12.61		31.12.62		Change	
	£	£	£	£	£	£
Fixed assets						
Premises, at cost		2,380		2,510		+130
Furniture, fittings and fixtures, at cost	1,780		1,830		+ 50	
less Depreciation	310	1,470	400	1,430	+ 90	− 40
		3,850		3,940		+ 90
Current assets						
Stock	1,001		1,580		+579	
Trade debtors	1,460		1,513		+ 53	
Cash	78	2,539	67	3,160	− 11	+621
		6,389		7,100		+711
less Current liabilities						
Trade creditors		2,234		2,640		+406
Net assets		4,155		4,460		+305
Ownership interest						
Share capital		3,000		3,000		—
Profit		1,155		1,460		+305
		4,155		4,460		+305

Whether the rise in cost is a reasonable one having regard to all the circumstances for the two years we cannot tell without further investigation. Again, the existence of earlier estimates may help us. In the final analysis, however, we must go behind the figures and study the circumstances of the changes.

It is useful at this point to examine the relationship between cost of sales and sales; this relationship can be expressed either in the form of the ratio of cost of sales to sales, or of the ratio of gross profit to sales. It is often more convenient to use the latter ratio, as business men tend to think in terms of this. In our example the ratio of gross profit to sales is approximately 20% in 1961 and 19% in 1962, as Table 9.1 shows. This change might be due to one or more of a number of causes. For example, it could have been caused by a rise in the average cost of goods purchased in relation to the average price of goods sold; it would then be necessary to ask why this had happened: the selling departments might be under-pricing or the buying department might have been less successful than before. Or the fall could be due to the loss or theft of stock so that what appeared to be the cost of sales

TABLE 9.2

RATIOS

Stock turnover rate[1]		
cost of sales/stock	$8,200/\ 1,001 = 8\cdot2$	$9,200/\ 1,580 = 5\cdot8$
Debtor turnover rate[1]		
sales/debtors	$10,200/\ 1,460 = 7\cdot0$	$11,400/\ 1,513 = 7\cdot5$
Creditor turnover rate[1]		
purchases/creditors	$8,350/\ 2,234 = 3\cdot7$	$9,779/\ 2,640 = 3\cdot7$
Current ratio		
current assets/current liabilities	$2,539/\ 2,234 = 1\cdot14$	$3,160/\ 2,640 = 1\cdot20$
Liquid ratio		
debtors + cash/current liabilities	$1,538/\ 2,234 = 0\cdot69$	$1,580/\ 2,640 = 0\cdot60$
Ratio of ownership interest to total claims		
capital + profit/capital + profit + liabilities	$4,155/\ 6,389 = 0\cdot65$	$4,460/\ 7,100 = 0\cdot63$
Ratio of net profit to average ownership interest		
net profit/$\frac{1}{2}$ (opening capital + opening profit + closing capital + closing profit)	$450/\frac{1}{2}(3,900+4,155)$ $= 11\cdot2\%$	$470/\frac{1}{2}(4,155+4,460)$ $= 10\cdot9\%$

1 The inverse gives, as a fraction of a year, the average period of investment in stock, of credit given, or of credit received, as the case may be. The ratios are only first approximations because we are comparing the balance sheet data at a given moment of time with the profit and loss data for the whole of the preceding year.

was in part the value of stock lost or stolen. Or there might have been a change in the mix of stock sold, in the sense that proportionately more goods carrying lower percentage rates of gross profit had been sold in the second year. These possibilities are not exhaustive. Nor does it follow that a fall in the gross profit percentage is bad in itself. It is the total gross profit that is important. The elasticity of demand may be such that total net revenue is increased by reductions in prices.

There is a lesson here that we must apply whenever we examine accounting data, namely that there is seldom a unique explanation of a given type of change. Accounting data rarely give us a definite answer to questions, but they can often suggest lines of investigation. It should be noted, too, that if, for example, a gross profit percentage has not changed it does not necessarily mean that there should be no investigation. Failure to change may mean that something that has been planned has not happened, or that two changes have happened in opposite directions, one tending to raise the percentage and one tending to lower it, so that the final percentage is unchanged. Nevertheless, there is a presumption that further investigation is not necessary if the percentage is unchanged, provided that this is what was expected.

Overhead expenses

In the next section of the profit and loss account are the various overhead expenses relating to different activities of the business. It is characteristic of such expenses that they are unlikely in the short run to change in direct proportion to the change in sales, whereas the cost of sales will often vary in direct proportion with sales, and is in any case likely to be much more sensitive to changes in sales. Even so, it is usually of some interest to relate each head of overhead expense to the level of sales. This is particularly true of the selling and distribution expenses, the size of which may reasonably be expected to be more closely correlated with the level of sales revenue than the other expenses. In our example, it can be seen by inspection that administrative expenses, and expenses of selling and distribution, have risen, though less proportionately than sales. A full interpretation of the increases would require, as usual, a more detailed investigation. However, if the business is growing, as the rise in sales suggests may be the case, it is not unreasonable to expect a gradual increase in such expenses. If, on the other hand, the rise in sales and cost of sales is due to rising prices, it can be expected that administrative expenses and the other expenses will also rise, but possibly at a slower rate, since they will consist of such items as salaries and rents.

Financial expenses have risen much more than in proportion to the other changes. The main items under this head are likely to be interest charges and, possibly, cash discounts to customers. If the business is expanding, we might indeed expect that more finance would be needed and that interest charges might rise. We shall defer further consideration of this item until we have examined some of the balance sheet changes.

The total of the overhead expenses has risen by £180. The net profit therefore has risen by only £20, the increase of £200 in gross profit having been almost absorbed by the rise in those expenses. The percentage of net profit to sales has in consequence fallen from 4·4 to 4·1.

Fixed assets

We now turn to the balance sheets. The first item is that of premises. Here there is an increase, over the two years, of £130. A change of this kind may be important when the future profitability of a business is under consideration. Increases in some or all of the various classes of fixed assets may suggest that future profitability, as new assets come into use, is likely to be greater than that shown in the current profit and loss account. On the other hand, it is also possible for such increases to lag behind the increase in profitability. A business may be able in the short run to increase its activity, and report higher profits, by straining its resources – over-running machinery and so on – in a way not possible in the longer run.

The next item is the furniture, fittings, and fixtures. Here there is a net fall of £40. This is compounded of an increase of £50 in the original cost and an increase of £90 in the depreciation. This tells the reader that there has been expenditure of £50 on the assets in question during the year (after deducting receipts from assets sold, if any). So far as it suggests anything, the change points to growth in the scale of the business, especially when taken in conjunction with the expenditure on premises, and this may imply growth in the profit in future, as noted above.

The increase in the depreciation figure merely reflects the fact that the assets existing at the beginning of the year are nearer to the end of their useful life; and the figure may include some allowance for fall in value of the new assets bought during the second year.

We know already that the balance sheet value of the fixed assets is not a good guide to the current realizable value of the assets in the market. The balance sheet does, however, remind us that the assets in question exist; this at least gives us the opportunity to make further enquiries about their value. We might think this desirable, for example, if it seemed possible that the company would be liquidated in the near future, if we were considering what security the company could offer for loans, or if we were attempting to estimate the rate of return being earned on the current value of the business's assets.

Current assets

We now come to the current assets. There has been a substantial increase in stock, a small increase in trade debtors, and a small fall in cash. We might well have expected increases in both stock and debtors, since we already know from the profit and loss account that there has been an increase in sales. One expects that to sell more one will have to carry more stock and, if the whole or part of the sales are on credit, that the trade debtors will tend to be higher too. The drop in cash is also not unexpected, since an expansion in business is likely to drain cash off into other types of asset; we have already seen that there has been expenditure on fixed assets in addition to the increase in stock and trade debtors. The fact that the cash balance seems to be rather low need not in itself cause us alarm, for it may be that the balance sheet date is one at which the cash balance is normally low. The drop as compared with last year is perhaps rather more significant. It is true that the change appears small. But it is significant as a percentage; if we were concerned with the same percentage fall in a cash balance of, say, £1,000,000, the drop would be over £140,000. If the fall continues at the same annual rate for two or three years, it may be necessary to raise additional finance. It may not be too early to begin thinking how this will be done.

Turnover ratios

It is useful to consider the growth of stock and trade debtors in relation to the increase in the sales; one way of making the position clearer is to relate these figures each year to the cost of sales, and to the sales, respectively. For example, in Table 9.2 we have calculated what is sometimes called the 'stock turnover rate', that is, the ratio of the annual cost of sales to stock. The cost of sales represents the value, based on purchase price, of the goods that have been sold. Stock is valued at cost or lower market value, and in any given business the amount that is held should generally bear a fairly constant relationship to the amount that is sold. There may of course be changes, depending upon the type of goods that are being sold and the way in which the business is developing; but if there are changes it is interesting to know how large they are and why they occur. In this case we notice that the ratio has dropped from 8·2 in the first year to 5·8

6

in the second. In other words the stock held at the balance sheet date has risen considerably in relation to the sales for the year. A 5·8 rate can be expressed in another way by saying that stock is 'turning over' during the year approximately once every two months on average.[1] If the ratio had been exactly six, this would have implied that one-sixth of the value, taken at cost, of the year's sales was held in stock at the end of the year. It will be noted that we are not here comparing the stock at a given moment of time with the rate of sales at that time; we are comparing stock at the end of the year with the sales for the year valued at cost price. Our measure is therefore a fairly crude one; nevertheless it can give us useful information. The fact that the ratio has fallen may suggest, for example, that the business is expected to expand even faster in the following year and that stock has been increased for this reason. Alternatively, however, it may indicate that mistakes have been made in buying and that an unusually large amount of unsaleable stock is now held. In any case the change calls for investigation unless the reader of the accounts already knows why it has happened. If he was expecting this kind of change, this will confirm his expectations. In either case he will have gained something from studying the accounts.

The debtor turnover rate is calculated in the same way, except that here we compare the total debtors at the end of the year with the sales figure. The debtors figure represents the amounts due from customers in respect of the sales price of goods they have bought and it is therefore appropriate to compare it with the selling value of the goods rather than the cost. Here the ratios are 7·0 and 7·5 respectively. The rise may mean that customers are paying more quickly, or that more customers are paying cash and fewer are buying on credit terms. However, it is the sales towards the end of the year that are responsible for the debts still outstanding at the balance sheet date, and the rise could be due to a change in the time pattern of sales during the year. The ratio is an important figure, and a significant change may suggest serious developments. For example, a big fall in this ratio might suggest that debtors were paying very slowly owing to deterioration in the system of collection or deterioration in the general conditions of trade, or that sales were being forced by selling to people

[1] $12/5·8 = 2·1$.

whose credit was bad. A rise in the ratio could imply that business was being conducted more efficiently, debts being collected more quickly; but the quicker collection might have a cost: it might mean that additional cash discounts had to be granted to the debtors to encourage prompt payment, thus increasing financial expenses, or that customers were being annoyed by pressure to pay quickly. In some circumstances such a rise could mean the business was in financial difficulties and was having to take every possible step to raise money.

Finance and liquidity

The total of the assets has risen by £711. The remaining sections of the balance sheet will tell us how this increase has been financed. We look first at the current liabilities. These have increased by £406. This, too, might have been expected, for we have been buying more goods, and it is likely therefore that more will be owing to creditors at the end of the year. Again, we can get some idea of what is happening by comparing the ratio of trade creditors at the end of each year to the purchases. (We must use purchases and not cost of sales, for there have been stock changes.) This ratio has remained constant at 3·7 (Table 9.2) and suggests therefore that no enquiry is necessary. If, for example, the ratio had risen, it would have meant that additional finance was being obtained from creditors by deferring payment for a longer period than before. This might be the result of buying different kinds of goods, or buying from different creditors, but it could also indicate that the business was finding it more difficult to raise money and was attempting to obtain more finance from its trade creditors. In this case the cost of postponement might be the sacrifice of cash discounts – possibly equivalent to a relatively high rate of interest – that would otherwise be obtained on payment of the creditors. This too, therefore, is an important ratio to watch.

The importance of liquidity, that is, the relation of the cash resources presently available, or likely to become available in the near future, to the cash that will be needed in the near future to meet liabilities and buy assets, leads to the calculation of two other ratios. The first, sometimes called the current ratio, is the ratio of current assets to current liabilities. It will be seen from

Table 9.2 that in our example this ratio has risen slightly, from 1·14 to 1·20. This indicates a slightly less tight liquid position. It should, however, be considered in relation to another ratio, the liquid ratio, the relation of the 'quick' assets (debtors and cash) to current liabilities. Stock may not be quickly realizable without a substantial price sacrifice. Debtors on the other hand can usually be turned into cash fairly quickly. Hence the liquid ratio gives us a better idea than the current ratio of the extent to which we should be squeezed if we had to pay the creditors off quickly. The liquid ratio has dropped from 0·69 to 0·60. This suggests that the company has become slightly less liquid. That the current ratio has risen is due to the fact that there has been a substantial increase in stock. This change may be significant. The examination of the two ratios draws our attention to it.

There are no definite rules that can tell us whether given ratios are correct. It is sometimes said that the current ratio should not be less than 2 and that the liquid ratio should not be less than 1, but it is doubtful whether this statement has much general significance. In some business, for example, it will be perfectly normal to finance much of the stock by obtaining long periods of credit from the suppliers; where this is the case the current and liquid ratios are bound to be lower than where it is not. A business that buys all its stock on credit terms and sells only for cash may, quite reasonably, have a liquid ratio well below 1 and a current ratio not much above 1. On the other hand, it is true that, other things being equal, higher current and liquid ratios indicate greater financial strength – greater ability to meet a crisis. They also indicate, other things being equal again, lower profitability, since more permanent finance is tied up.[1] Changes in ratios are usually more significant than absolute levels, for they may suggest the kind of developments that are taking place.

As has already been indicated, the lower that it is possible to keep the current and liquid ratios, the more is the business economizing its liquid resources and the lower are its interest charges likely to be. On the other hand, it may be making sacrifices, in that it is offering cash discounts to its debtors to pay quickly, and abstaining from taking discounts from its creditors because it does not pay them quickly. We have already noticed

1 This means that more interest must be paid to longer term lenders or that more ownership finance must be provided per £ of profit.

in the profit and loss account that there has been a considerable increase in financial expenses during the year. As cash discounts given to debtors (less those received from creditors) will probably be classified under financial expenses, this increase might be explained by the kind of points we have just been making. Alternatively the increased interest during the year might be due to having to run an overdraft at the bank for some period during the year.

We have seen that £406 of the finance needed to obtain the increase in assets has come from an increase in trade creditors. The remainder comes from the increase of £305 in the shareholders' interest which has arisen because the 1961 profit has not been fully withdrawn from the business. Thus more than half of the additional finance has come from creditors as distinct from the ownership interest. It is interesting to calculate the ratio of the ownership interest to the total claims. This ratio is given in Table 9.2 as 0·65 in the first year and 0·63 in the second, the decrease being due to the point we have just made. This ratio is an indicator of the extent to which the business is financed by the owners as distinct from outside sources who would be able to press for payment to the point of legal action if the occasion arose. To this extent, therefore, the ratio is an indicator of the degree of risk that the owners might lose control of the business if there were a period of unsuccessful trading, in which liquid resources were depleted, and additional finance could not be obtained.

Rate of return on investment

The final ratio in Table 9.2 is that of the net profit to the average ownership interest during the year. This ratio gives some idea of the rate of return that is being earned upon the capital invested in the business. As a rough approximation the ownership interest is taken as the average of the opening and closing figures. This calculation is of considerable economic significance. An owner of resources is interested in comparing the return on his resources in any particular use with the possible return in other uses. The ratio calculated as we have shown it does not give us a very accurate measure for this purpose, as it is based on balance sheet values of assets; these are not necessarily good measures of the market value of resources – what could be realized by transferring resources to other uses. However, it does give us a rough idea. This can be improved upon, if desired, by estimating more precisely the market values of the assets. More important, perhaps, changes in the ratio from year to year give us an idea of the development of the business from the point of view of the profitability of investing further resources. The ratio must be interpreted carefully, for, as we have already explained, there may be a time lag between the addition of fixed assets to the business and an increase in the return from their use. Nevertheless, taken over a period – preferably more than two years – changes in the ratio are of some significance. Furthermore, although the absolute level of the ratio must be interpreted cautiously, if it is *very* low (or *very* high) in relation to what one would expect when resources were used for other purposes, it may well be significant. For example, if the return is very high this may suggest that it would be profitable to invest more resources in the business. It may also suggest that there is danger from competition which will eventually tend to drive down the rate of return. (In an enterprise which wielded a fairly high degree of monopoly power a high return could indicate that this monopoly power was being used, though, for a number of reasons, this would not be conclusive.) If the return is very low, it suggests that it may be better to close down the business. But the ratio must only be used as a first approximation. If it suggests, because it is unduly high or low, that further inquiry is desirable, more careful valuations should be made of the assets, with particular reference to what they would realize if withdrawn from the business, and attention must be paid to lags of the type we have already indicated between investment and increase in profit. More careful investigation may then confirm the original conclusion or, alternatively, may suggest reasons why it should not be accepted.

We relate profit to average capital employed because normally the capital is growing throughout the year as the result of the profit accumulation, and it would be reasonable therefore to expect a lower absolute level of profit at the beginning than at the end of the year. This calculation is only a rough approximation, but it must be remembered that it is of the nature of this type of economic measurement that very fine estimates are not possible.

A figure to which some importance may be attached is the annual percentage growth in net profit (shown in Table 9.1 as 4·4%) and in dividends (which in this example was negative, the dividend of 1962 being lower than that for 1961). In more sophisticated analyses, taken over a number of years, these might be expressed as compound interest rates of growth in profit and dividend.

This completes our demonstration of the way in which accounting figures may be interpreted with the object of obtaining a clearer picture of the economic circumstances and changes that lie behind them. Our main object has been to demonstrate principles and methods of approach, rather than to provide an exhaustive discussion of all the different ways in which data of this kind can be analysed. Indeed it would hardly be possible to provide such a discussion, for there are an indefinitely large number of different ways in which this kind of analysis can be carried out. Nevertheless the ratios we have calculated are in fact very often used in practice, and probably provide as good an approach as any to the problem of interpreting any given set of accounts.

The comparison of accounting figures of different businesses or other organizations (such as hospitals), with the object of throwing light on their comparative efficiency, can be carried out in a similar way, and raises similar considerations. Special care is needed in drawing conclusions from such comparisons owing to the difficulty of being sure that like is being compared with like; activities similarly described in the accounting reports and manuals of procedure of various organizations often differ in reality.

APPENDIX

EXERCISES

Chapter 1

1.1 Draw up your personal balance sheet at the beginning of last week. Then list your personal transactions for the week so far as you can remember them, and prepare:

    (*a*) a cash statement

    (*b*) a statement of income, expenditure on consumption and saving

    (*c*) a closing balance sheet

1.2 Explain why an individual's saving in a period is not necessarily measured by the change in his cash holding in the same period. (Note that 'cash' includes coin, notes and money at the bank.)

Chapter 2

2.1 Construct an imaginary balance sheet for three of the organizations listed below, showing the classes of assets and liabilities, and the ownership claims, that you would expect to find, and inserting arbitrary values for each class:

    (*a*) a bus company

    (*b*) a retail grocer

    (*c*) a municipal swimming bath

    (*d*) a society for the abolition of taxation

    (*e*) a university college

(f) an aircraft manufacturer
(g) a film production company
(h) an atomic energy authority
(i) a bank

2.2 From the data given below, which refer to a wholesale business, prepare:

(a) an opening balance sheet as at 1 January 19—
(b) a set of double entry accounts, similar to those in Table 2.3
(c) a balance sheet as at 31 January 19—, using the closing balances obtained in (b)

Data:

Assets and liabilities at the opening of business on 1 January 19—

	£
Cash at bank	1,420
Trade debtors	410
Trade creditors	260
Stock	3,210

Transactions:

January	1	Stock purchased on credit	420
,,	5	Trade creditors paid by cheque	205
,,	10	Stock costing £560 sold on credit for	720
,,	17	Drawings by owner	100
,,	26	Rent of premises paid for month	40
,,	31	Wages paid for month	60

2.3 What are the fundamental rules of double entry?

Chapter 3

3.1 Using your solution to question 2.2, draw up a profit and loss report for January.

3.2 The figures given below comprise the double entry ledger accounts of a trading business for the first month of trading, before the insertion of the closing balances at the end of the month. You are required to insert the closing balances in the ledger accounts and prepare two sets of accounting reports for the owner. Each set should be in the form of a profit and loss account for the month, an appropriation account (where relevant) and a balance sheet at the end of the month. Prepare the first set on the assumption that the business belongs to a sole trader and the second set on the assumption that it is carried on as a limited company.

DOUBLE ENTRY ACCOUNTS

	Stock		Trade debtors		Cash at bank		Capital		Profit and loss	
	Dr £	Cr £	Dr £	Cr £	Dr £	Cr £	Dr £	Cr £	Dr £	Cr £
Cash paid in by owner					500			500		
Stock bought	300					300				
Stock sold on credit		200	300							100
Stock sold for cash		50			75					25
Wages paid						40			40	
Rent paid						45			45	
Withdrawn by owner						80	80			

3.3 What alternative meanings are given to the noun 'capital' in accounting?

Chapter 4

4.1 *A*, a doctor, has the following assets and liabilities relating to his medical practice on 1 January and 31 December 19—:

	1 Jan £	31 Dec £
Surgery equipment	2,765	2,936
Motor car	880	660
Stock of drugs	432	382
Due from Ministry	736	867
Due to creditors	95	69
Cash at bank	79	93

During the year his weekly drawings amounted in total to £1,632, but he paid into the practice bank account a £25 prize received from his private holding of Premium Bonds.

Prepare opening and closing balance sheets (i.e. at 1 Jan and 31 Dec) and compute the profit (or loss) of the practice for the year on the assumption that all the valuations may be accepted.

Hint: The profit must be the difference between the opening and closing capital, adjusted by money paid in or withdrawn by the owner of the practice. There is not enough information to permit the preparation of full double entry records.

4.2 Using the same opening data (i.e. at 1 January) as in question 1, but ignoring all other data in that question, prepare on the basis of the summarized information given below: (*a*) a set of double entry records for the year; (*b*) a profit and loss report for the year; and (*c*) a closing balance sheet at 31 December.

	£
Debt due from Ministry on 1 Jan received and paid into bank	736
Fees received from Ministry during year (in addition to the above item) and paid into the bank	1,475
Drugs bought from suppliers during year and paid for by cheque	324
Creditors at 1 Jan paid by cheque	95
Value of drugs (valued at cost) used in practice during year	443
Drugs bought from suppliers during year not paid for at 31 Dec	69
Fees due from Ministry not paid at 31 Dec	867
Loss in value ('depreciation') of motor car during year	220
Surgery equipment purchased and paid for by cheque during year	171
Drawings during year	1,607

4.3 The data given below relate to a small manufacturing company. From these prepare double entry records for the month, and appropriate accounting reports:

Assets and liabilities, 1 March 19—

	£
Stocks (valued at cost):	
Raw materials	560
Work in progress	227
Finished goods	281
Trade debtors	322
Trade creditors	169
Cash at bank	329

Equipment (valued at cost *less* an estimate of
loss in value due to wear and tear) 620
Share capital 2,000
Profit and loss account (credit) 170

Transactions:

			£
March	3	Sold goods costing £53 on credit	78
,,	6	Bought raw materials on credit	113
,,	7	Paid wages	22
,,	11	Received payment from debtors	162
,,	14	Paid wages	22
,,	16	Completed work on certain products, cost for balance sheet valuation being assessed at	93
,,	21	Paid wages	22
,,	23	Paid creditors	87
,,	24	Sold on credit stock costing £120 for	190
,,	28	Paid wages	22
,,	31	Paid monthly rent	30
		Paid dividend to shareholders	40

During the month raw materials costing £40 were taken out of
store for manufacturing purposes.

Half the wages and half the rent are assumed to add to the
value of work in progress. The remainder is written off as an
administrative expense to profit and loss account.

The loss in value of the equipment during the month is assessed
at £5. An equivalent amount of value is assumed to be added to
the work in progress.

Chapter 5

5.1 Draw up a set of T form ledger accounts for the example
at the beginning of Chapter 2. Use separate accounts for cost of
goods sold and for sales. Insert the closing balances and prepare
a trial balance.

5.2 Carry out a similar exercise to that in 5.1 with respect to
the data in Exercise 2.2 above.

5.3 Write out each debit and credit entry required by question
5.2 in the form of a journal entry.

5.4 Explain briefly the normal conventions used in the valuation, for business balance sheets, of the various kinds of stocks.

Chapter 6

6.1 *A* starts a business with a capital of £1,150. The business consists of buying automatic vending machines and selling confectionery through the machines.

A withdraws each year the whole of the profit shown by his accounts, but no more. His stock remains constant at £100 (at cost). He always pays cash for purchases. At the end of 5 years *A*'s balance sheet is as follows:

A

Balance Sheet, 31 December

	£		£	£
Capital	1,150	Automatic machines:		
		Cost	1,000	
		Depreciation	500	
			——	500
		Stock in machines		
		and in store	100	
		Cash at bank	550	
			——	650
	1,150			1,150

A tells you he cannot understand why his cash balance is so high when he has withdrawn all his profit each year.

Explain to him why this is.

6.2 At what period or periods during a business's life would you expect the needs for finance to be especially high? Explain your answer and if possible illustrate it with simple balance sheets.

6.3 *C* is a dentist. His practice balance sheets at the end of two successive years are:

	Year 1 £	Year 2 £		Year 1 £	Year 2 £
Capital	1,560	2,050	Equipment (at cost)	1,320	1,700
Creditors	70	120	Fees owing	160	390
			Cash at bank	150	80
	1,630	2,170		1,630	2,170

'Capital' in this case includes original capital paid in and profits not withdrawn.

In Year 2 the profit was £1,390 of which £900 was withdrawn during the year for personal needs.

C complains that there is now not enough money at the bank to allow him to enjoy the balance of his profit.

Write a short letter to him explaining the financial position of the practice.

Chapter 7

7.1 A firm's trial balance on 1 January is as follows:

	£	£
Capital		1,000
Stock	500	
Debtors	300	
Creditors		200
Cash at bank	150	
Equipment (cost)	460	
Depreciation provision		210
	1,410	1,410

During January and February sales are expected to be at the rate of £200 per month and thereafter at £300 per month. Purchases will be at the rate of £160 per month throughout the months January to April.

Debtors' balances are due during the second calendar month and creditors' balances during the third calendar month after the end of the calendar month in which the sales or purchases, as the case may be, occur. All sales and purchases are for credit.

General expenses of all kinds will require a monthly cash outlay of £30.

In March new equipment is to be bought for £350, payable at once in cash.

The owner will withdraw £20 per month for personal use.

Calculate the cash balance at the end of April assuming that all receipts and payments occur on their expected due date, and prove your answer by preparing a balance sheet at 30 April.

Hint: Prepare double entry accounts as they will appear if the assumption is correct.

7.2 *A* is starting up a new business on 1 January 19—. He asks you to calculate for him his estimated profit during the first half-year. He provides the following information:

	£
Annual rent of premises, payable quarterly in arrear, first payment due on 31 March	3,600
Cash outlay on equipment – payable 15 January	3,700
payable 15 March	5,400

Monthly planned purchases of stock for re-sale (estimated cost):

January	15,000
February	25,000
March to June inclusive (per month)	10,000

All stock is bought on two months' credit.

Monthly planned sales (at estimated selling prices):

January	6,000
February	8,000
March	11,000
April–June inclusive (per month)	12,000

Planned selling price each month is on average 20% above cost.

All sales are on one month's credit. No bad debts or arrears of payments are expected.

Monthly cash outlay on general expenses including salaries is expected to be   480

Depreciation of equipment in the first half-year is estimated at 5% of initial cost.

A will pay £30,000 cash into the business. He does not plan to withdraw any money from the business during the year.

Required: (*a*) Budgeted trading and profit and loss account for the half-year, and closing balance sheet, in a form suitable for presentation to management.

(*b*) A statement showing the maximum finance (other than that provided by trade creditors) that will be needed during the half-year, and the amount by which *A*'s paid-in capital exceeds this figure. State the date on which the maximum amount given will be needed. (Assume that all receipts and payments in any given month will occur on the last day of the month in which they fall due.)

Hint: As the question asks for the maximum figure of cash needed (which requires ascertainment of the date of the minimum debit balance) it will be necessary to compute the balance of the bank account at the end of each month.

7.3 At the beginning of 1960 a small shipping firm, owned by an individual owner-manager, has the following assets and liabilities:

	£
Motor vessel (at cost)	200,000
Stock of sea-going stores	16,000
Cash at bank	15,000
Debtors (for freight)	14,000
Creditors (for harbour dues and other expenses of voyages)	19,000

During 1960 the following transactions (which have been summarized) occur:

	£
Cheques and cash received for freight in 1960 including £14,000 from the debtors at 1.1.60	86,000
Payments from bank for expenses of voyages including £19,000 to the creditors at 1.1.60	28,000
Payments from bank for office and general expenses	11,000
Payments from bank for purchase of stores	26,000
Cash drawn from bank by owner for personal use	2,000
Harbour dues and other voyage expenses incurred in 1960, but not paid for at 31.12.60	14,000

At 31.12.60 the stock of stores held was valued (on cost basis) at £13,800. The difference between this figure and stock previously held and bought during the year is an addition to the cost of voyages during the year.

The depreciation of the ship is estimated on the basis of a straight-line fall in value, over a period of 20 years, to a zero residual value. At 31.12.59 the ship was 2 years old.

The ship had just begun a voyage at 31.12.60. Expenses of that voyage (included in the expenses shown above) amounting to £3,500 are to be treated as an asset (like 'work in progress' in a manufacturing business) at balance sheet date. No revenue from this voyage has yet been received or included in the above figures.

Required: Balance sheet at 31.12.60 and profit and loss account for 1960.

Show all working calculations.

Hint: Start by calculating the opening capital. Then use T accounts and prepare a trial balance as at 31.12.60.

7.4 Prepare a profit and loss statement for 1957, and a closing balance sheet, from the following data relating to the business of *R*, a sole trader:

Summary of bank account for 1957

	£		£
Debtors for goods	4,410	Balance, 1 January	660
Sale of business invest-		Creditors for goods	2,900
ment	1,820	General expenses	980
		Drawings	760
		Balance, 31 December	930
	6,230		6,230

The ledgers that were kept show the following balances:

Close of business 31 December 1956	£
Debtors for goods sold	5,820
Creditors for goods bought	1,640
Furniture, fixtures and fittings	1,890
Investment	1,800
Petty cash	40
Close of business 31 December 1957	
Debtors for goods sold	6,590
Creditors for goods bought	2,100
Furniture, fixtures and fittings	1,890
Petty cash	60

The depreciation rate for the furniture, fixtures and fittings is 10% on the opening balance each year. Stock in trade at 31 December 1956 was £2,010 and at 31 December 1957, £2,830.

7.5 The following accounting information for 19— relates to the Brightmouth-on-Sea Municipal Opera House:

Ledger balances at 31 December: £

Surplus on income and expenditure account (as at previous 1 January)[1]   1,252

1 This is the equivalent of the capital account of a sole trader.

	£
Musical, stage and other equipment (as at previous 1 January)	1,919
Stocks of food and drink for the restaurant as at 1 January	590
Bank overdraft	530
Liability in respect of money paid for advance bookings	187
Sundry creditors	762
House receipts from sale of tickets (other than advance bookings)	6,732
Catering sales	3,416
Catering purchases	2,437
Salaries and wages (of which £500 refer to the restaurant)	4,938
General expenses, including rent, insurance, interest, etc.	1,762
Expenditure on productions during year	1,233

Additional information:

Stocks of food and drink as at 31 December	229

10% is written off the musical and other equipment annually.

Required: Annual accounts (income and expenditure account and balance sheet) for 19—.

7.6 Another business has the same balance sheet at the beginning of a given year as in Example 8 of Chapter 7.

The following forecasts are made for this business for the year:

	£
Cash expenditure on replacement of equipment worn out (fully depreciated in the accounts at the beginning of year, i.e. reduced to zero value)	1,100
Sales (including sales of £550 not paid for at end of the year)	4,800
Purchases (including purchases of £650 not paid for at end of year)	3,200
Stock (at cost) at end of year	600
General expenses (all paid in cash)	890
Depreciation	310
Owner's drawings during year	420

Required: (1) Advise the owner:

(*a*) On the expected financial (i.e. cash) position during the year.

(*b*) What special action, if any, this position calls for.

(2) Do you think there are any important differences between the situations in this question and Example 8 of Chapter 7 from the point of view of financing? Give your reasons.

7.7 *A* Ltd. is a small furniture-making company. Its financial position at 1 January 19— is as follows:

Assets:	£
Machinery and tools (original cost)	6,000
Provision for depreciation (deduction from asset)	3,000
Stock of wood (cost)	4,000
Work in progress	6,000
Finished furniture	5,000
Trade debtors	2,000
Cash at bank	1,000

Claims:	
Trade creditors	1,000
Share capital	15,000
Profit and loss account	5,000

The transactions for the year following, summarized, are:	
Sales to customers on credit	20,000
Purchases of wood from suppliers on credit	4,000
Cash received from customers	21,000
Cash paid to suppliers	3,000
Cost of wood drawn from stock for manufacture	5,000
Cost of furniture finished (calculated as stated below)	13,000
Cost of furniture sold (calculated as stated below)	15,000
Cash paid for productive wages	9,000
Cash paid for general manufacturing expenses	1,000
Cash paid for general administrative expenses	2,000
Amount owing to landlord for rent of workshop up to end of year, unpaid at 31 December	1,000
Cash dividend paid to shareholders	1,000

Note: The company values its work in progress and finished goods stock at the direct cost of production (cost of wood and productive labour only). All other expenditure is treated as current expense for the period to which it relates. Depreciation of machinery, etc., is assessed at 10% per annum on cost.

Required: (*a*) Set of double entry accounts in T form and closing trial balance.

(*b*) Final accounts for the year for report to the shareholders (balance sheet, profit and loss account and appropriation account).

Chapter 8

8.1 A firm keeps a detailed creditors ledger, controlled by a creditors control account, and a detailed stock ledger controlled by a stock control account. The stock ledger is kept in quantity as well as value.

On 1 March the list of the detailed creditors ledger balances is as follows:

Suppliers	£
A	386
B	15

The detailed stock ledger balances are:

Goods	Items	£
X	18	182
Y	1	15

During March:

(*a*) B supplies 10 items of good type X at £95, and 1 item of type Y at £12.

(*b*) A's account is settled in full.

(*c*) A later supplies 4 items of good type X at £38, and 1 item of type Z at £18.

(*d*) C supplies goods of type Y, 6 items, at £73.

(*e*) 9 items of type X, valued at £86, are issued from store for despatch to a customer.

Required: Show the creditors control account and the stock control account for March, and prove the correctness of each by extracting lists of the detailed creditors ledger and detailed stock ledger (value) balances. Draw a diagram showing the flow of information to the clerks or machine operators responsible for the various jobs.

8.2 You, as accountant of a wholesale grocer, are asked by your chief:

(a) What did we pay in rent last year?

(b) How long have we been dealing with our customer John Brown? Does he pay regularly?

(c) How much cash have we at the bank, how much do we owe to creditors and how much do debtors owe us?

(d) How many lb. of cayenne pepper have we in stock?

Where would you find the answers to each of these questions:

(1) If the accounts were fully up to date;

(2) If the accounting work was a month in arrear?

8.3 The double entry accounting system of a business includes a creditors control account which controls a subordinate creditors ledger.

At 31 December the trial balance debit and credit totals (based on control account balances) are:

Dr	Cr
£	£
6,126	6,245

The credit side of the trial balance includes £862 as the balance of the creditors control account. The list of the subordinate creditors ledger balances adds up, however, to £887.

The following errors are found:

(a) The balance of W. Smith, a creditor, has been brought down as £8 instead of £18 in the detailed creditors ledger.

(b) £162 that has been debited to equipment account represents a payment for rent.

(c) When a batch of suppliers' invoices was totalled in order to provide the figure for the control account, the amounts of two invoices, together totalling £35, were omitted; the creditors ledger machine operator posted the invoices accurately to the subordinate ledger, but failed to check the total of the detail postings against the above control total and the supervisor failed to notice this. The stock ledger and the stock control account were posted correctly, but in neither case was the total checked against the original, incorrect control total.

(d) Invoices for goods supplied. costing £167, have not been received. No record of the purchase or of the receipt of the goods has reached the accounting system, but the goods are in the store.

(e) In the account for rent, £77 for rent paid has accidentally been entered on the credit side of the account.

There are no other errors. You may assume that the closing stock value is obtained from the balance of the stock control account after crediting the cost of sales, the latter being independently determined.

Required: (1) What is the correct trial balance total?

(2) What is the correct amount of the balance of the creditors control account and of the list of the detailed creditors ledger balances?

(3) If the net profit before correcting errors was £500, what is it after the corrections have been made?

In your answer show separately the effect of (*a*), (*b*), (*c*), (*d*), and (*e*) under each head (1), (2), and (3).

Hint: Begin by drawing a flow chart.

8.4   In a given business the sales accounting is organized so that the debtors' transactions are recorded in detail in a subordinate sales ledger controlled by a debtors control account in the general ledger. The general ledger includes the whole of the formal double entry system.

A trial balance is extracted from the general ledger and is found not to balance. After investigation the following errors are found:

(*a*) A copy sales invoice for £30 had been mislaid before it reached the accounting department. (The copy invoices provide the sales posting information.)

(*b*) The machinist posted a cash receipt of £67 to the detailed sales ledger as £76 and failed to notice that the total amount of cash receipts posted by her to the detailed ledger did not agree with the initial control total of the cash receipts summary (which would agree with the control account posting).

(*c*) The discount on sales transactions listed with the cash receipts data was £80. A fly's leg stuck to the paper after the sales ledger machinist had made, and agreed, her detail postings, and the general ledger clerk, when making his general ledger control account postings, read the figure as £180.

(d) The debit side of the debtors control account in the general ledger was cast ('added up') incorrectly, the total appearing £10 greater than it should.

Required: (1) State the net difference (between debit and credit totals) on the general ledger trial balance, stating whether it arose from excess debit or excess credit.

(2) State the difference, if any, between the sum of the individual sales ledger balances and the debtors control account in the general ledger, indicating whether the former shows greater net debit or net credit than the latter.

(3) State clearly what adjustments must be made in the general ledger to correct it.

(4) What difference, if any, to the profit do the corrections make?

Give your calculations, showing in each section of the answer the respective effects of (a), (b), (c), and (d), and the net result.

Answers must be set out clearly.

Hint: You are unlikely to get the answer to this question right unless you start by visualizing the step-by-step accounting procedure, e.g. by drawing a flow chart.

8.5 Explain clearly and carefully, making use of diagrams if you think they will be helpful, an accounting procedure for the collection, recording, and classification (i.e. the data-processing) of information relating to the following business activities. Show the procedure from the point where the original data becomes available to the completion of the formal double entry records.

(1) Sale of goods on credit.
(2) Purchase of goods on credit.
(3) Receipt and payment of cash (all receipts being banked and all payments being made by cheque).
(4) Receipt, store, and issue of goods for sale.

Chapter 9

9.1 Give an interpretation of the following figures, summarized from the accounting reports of a company for two successive years:

	£000	
	Year 1	*Year 2*
Sales	1,950	2,290
Cost of sales	1,370	1,640
Office and general expenses	246	308
Travellers' commission and expenses	21	26
Running and maintenance costs, and depreciation, of delivery trucks	13	16
Interest on bank loan	20	—
	1,670	1,990
Net profit	280	300
Taxation	120	130
	160	170
Undistributed profit from previous year	260	380
	420	550
Dividends on shares	40	80
Profit retained in business	380	470
Property, plant, and equipment		
Balance from previous year	850	1,000
Additions *less* sales	150	260
	1,000	1,260
Depreciation	400	490
	600	770
Other fixed assets (net)	70	90
	670	860
Stocks	630	830
Trade debtors	570	690
Cash at bank and in hand	280	380
	2,150	2,760

	£000	
	Year 1	*Year 2*
Share capital	680	1,000
Profit	380	470
	1,060	1,470
Long term loans	390	480
Trade creditors	700	810
	2,150	2,760

SHORT READING LIST

Accounting as an academic subject is still in its infancy, and well-written books dealing with principles are still few in number. Care in selection is especially desirable, therefore. For an introductory book written from a rather more traditional viewpoint than this one, the reader might try

> S. W. Rowland and B. Magee, *Accounting* (Gee, London)

On company accounting

> S. W. Rowland, *Principles of Accounting* (Donnington & Cassell, London) is perhaps as good as any British text at present available.

For an introduction to management accounting, see

> H. C. Edey, *Business Budgets and Accounts* (Hutchinson, London)

There are now a number of quite good American and Australian introductory texts, though the reader must be prepared for some differences in terminology and must remember that differences in company and tax law will affect some of the detail. The following, all of which include introductions to management as well as financial accounting, are useful:

> R. N. Anthony, *Management Accounting* (Irwin, Illinois)
> H. Bierman, *Financial and Managerial Accounting* (Macmillan, New York)
> M. J. Gordon and G. Shillinglaw, *Accounting: A Management Approach* (Irwin, Illinois)
> C. T. Horngren, *Accounting for Management Control* (Prentice-Hall, New Jersey)
> R. Mathews, *Accounting for Economists* (Cheshire, Melbourne)

For a general introduction to business finance, read

> F. W. Paish, *Business Finance* (Pitman, London)

On the legal side of company finance

L. C. B. Gower, *Modern Company Law* (Stevens, London) is a first-class book, readable and instructive.

For further study of the theoretical foundations of financial and management accounting, and in particular of problems of cost, income measurement and valuation, see

- W. T. Baxter and S. Davidson, *Studies in Accounting Theory* (Sweet & Maxwell, London)
- D. Solomons, *Studies in Costing* (Sweet & Maxwell, London)
- J. W. Bennett, J. McB. Grant and R. H. Parker, *Topics in Business Finance and Accounting* (Cheshire, Melbourne)
- A. J. Merrett and A. Sykes, *The Finance and Analysis of Capital Projects* (Longmans, London)
- J. T. S. Porterfield, *Investment Decisions and Capital Costs* (Prentice-Hall, New Jersey)

For financial control in large organisations, see

- D. Solomons, *Divisional Performance: Measurement and Control* (Financial Executives Research Foundation, New York)

On the history of accounting, see

- A. C. Littleton and B. S. Yamey, *Studies in the History of Accounting* (Sweet & Maxwell, London)
- B. S. Yamey, H. C. Edey and H. W. Thomson, *Accounting in England and Scotland 1543–1800* (Sweet & Maxwell, London)

For an introduction to computers and computer programming, see

- T. W. McRae, *Introduction to Business Computer Programming* (Gee, London)
- —— *The Impact of Computers on Accounting* (Wiley, London)
- R. K. Livesley, *An Introduction to Automatic Digital Computers* (Cambridge University Press)
- J. F. Davison, *Programming for Digital Computers* (Business Publications and Batsford, London)

INDEX

The index does not cover the Appendix or the Short Reading List

181